In remembe
Charge You

Swift
x-mas 1961,

CHRISTOLOGY AND PERSONALITY

CHRISTOLOGY
AND
PERSONALITY

BY

Surjit Singh

FOREWORD BY
Nels F. S. Ferré

THE WESTMINSTER PRESS
Philadelphia

LIBRARY OF CONGRESS CATALOG CARD No. 61–6102

PRINTED IN THE UNITED STATES OF AMERICA

To

INDIRA

Companion of a Common Voyage

CONTENTS

FOREWORD BY NELS F. S. FERRÉ

K. R. POPPER, a British philosopher, has suggested that there are two basic kinds of thinkers: the Pythagorean and the Ionian. The Pythagorean argues from the authority of a master and a sacred tradition of interpretation. There can be dispute as to what the master said and how to interpret it, and there can also be defense of his position, but there should be no real questioning of it. The moving spirit of Pythagorean thinking is acceptance of authority. Pythagoras, for instance, taught that there were only rational numbers. The discovery of irrational numbers became a matter of embarrassment to his disciples, a scandal to be hidden from conscious view. When one of the disciples, Hippasos of Metapontum, dared to air this fact that according to orthodoxy should not be there, the other disciples took him out and drowned him. Surjit Singh will never be drowned! He is passionately a disciple of the orthodox Christian tradition and has argued only to discover the true faith and to defend it.

The other tradition that Popper suggested, the Ionian, took the road of open inquiry and never sought any conclusion that was not immediately subject to new inquiry and to further truth. The Pythagorean position represents the givenness of Christian revelation with no need for new knowledge, since Christ is the final revelation. The Biblical and historic witness concerning him is also authoritative and mostly in need of being rightly established. The Ionian approach is represented

9

by modern science in its restless, rootless seeking and never
finding any final truth. For some, the Pythagorean approach
would stand for the nature of faith resting in authority, while
the Ionian would stand for the nature of fact, never affording
saving truth in which to rest. Professor Singh is a man of faith!

When I first read Dr. Singh's position on Christ a few years
ago, I was so deeply impressed by it that I have been advocat-
ing ever since his being widely and thoroughly read. It is therefore a privilege for me to introduce this new book on Christology for American readers. I do so wholeheartedly in spite
of some remarks I have to make. I still believe that Dr. Singh
has a solid and important position to offer on the central Christian doctrine. Obviously I was taken aback when I discovered
that this new writing has produced a work that I believe to be
far more orthodox than the New Testament!

Before I discuss the reasons for my desire to spread the gospel of this book I want to indicate why I call Dr. Singh's work
more orthodox by far than the New Testament. Dr. Schlink, of
Heidelberg, has asserted that there is a one-way street from the
New Testament to Nicaea and Chalcedon. There is no going
back from the kind of interpretative unity given to Christology
by the major ecumenical councils to find the same unity in the
original Biblical source material. Dr. Singh, nevertheless, finds
such unity in the Bible and I believe that it is imposed. I do
not object to his uninhibited exegesis. Many theologians can
exhibit that! Tillich finds that at no point Jesus tried to be God
and that by accepting his finiteness fully he became transparent
to the ultimate dimension of essence. Contrariwise, Singh
creates a rhapsody of orthodoxy in Jesus' awareness of his
deity.

Both Tillich and Singh, in my opinion, fail to be open to the
more complicated and even contradictory material of the New
Testament. But both are using the Bible to establish a position.
I have a feeling that Tillich comes closer to the critical historian's picture of Jesus at his best, but this is not the place to
more than mention the problems I feel. How simply Dr. Singh

places Christ on the side of God rather than of creation in Col., ch. 1, or finds orthdoxy in Phil., ch. 2, or even runs roughshod over clear manuscript evidence that attributes the being born not of blood, flesh, or man, but of the will of God to Jesus and not to the plural believers. Passage after passage I followed the author's benign nod at scholarly problems and then his coming out via some scholar or other for the kind of conservative scholarship that sees unity throughout the whole New Testament except for development of interpretation. He even denies that there are Christologies in the New Testament. Dr. Singh will never be drowned by the other disciples. He is a dependable Pythagorean.

He has distinguished precedent, however, for this kind of interpretation. Long ago Athanasius, for instance, in arguing against the Arians (*Third Oration Against the Arians*) granted that they had passages that taken by themselves seemed to support their position and seemed contradictory of the emerging orthodox interpretation of Christ. But, he charged, they did not observe the *skopos* of interpretation; they failed to work within the sense of the whole, the total context, the full pattern of meaningfulness within which alone all the texts began to make sense. Thus Athanasius claimed for the New Testament a unified Christology for whoever was willing to receive the total truth of God's revelation in the Christ as reported in the Bible.

Athanasius, of course, lived before modern critical scholarship. But even today it is evidently possible with honesty and competence to put on the glasses of orthodoxy and read the Biblical accounts as a unity, even on the subject of Christ. And such reading not only is Fundamentalist but is becoming an ecumenical pastime and indeed the sign and seal of recognizing ecumenical Biblical scholarship.

I wonder wistfully whether the church of Christ will not be stronger and more resolute if it can put behind itself once for all the debilitating critical scholarship that confused faith and sapped conviction. By avoiding certain verses, by reading others within an orthodox perspective, and by aiming at piety and unity, many modern scholars, dividing the responsibility, can achieve some kind of intangible *status quo* consensus that can become the solid foundation for orthodox dogmatics.

Surjit Singh has achieved a unity of Biblical, historical, and systematic materials that can be of high help to the ecumenical church in its strong endeavor to build again a unity of the faith. This book may signal the incoming of the new generations of postcritical scholars who have left behind the thorny problems that have torn many of us older interpreters who are still caught in the critical tradition of an unregenerate scholarship. I hail the publication of this book as the resurgence of conservative theology on the part of one who has known thoroughly the critical tradition.

Some of us believe, however, that such unity is Biblicism, an artificially constructive unity in the light of a later doctrine, and prefer to such Biblicism the open Bible of the fallible record to the infallible God whose love became declaratively known in Jesus Christ through his teaching, life, death, and resurrection. Dr. Singh starts with the resurrection, he says, and in the light of its fact understands the developing unity of Christology in the New Testament. But why not see the unity of God's love consummatorily present in the Person who lived, died, and was raised in triumph from the dead?

The distinctive and determinative motif of Agape, Dr. Singh never develops at all. As a matter of fact he grants with the critics of the New Testament that there is no new teaching in it. I have spent a lifetime openly seeking for Agape outside the Biblical faith and especially outside the New Testament. In its full personal and eternal meaning I have never found it anywhere else. And if God is Agape in Christ, the eternally faithful, what more do we need? Then we can have a firm faith with an open mind. We can be Pythagorean and Ionian in a way that fulfills both by giving faith the open mind and the open mind the fulfilling faith.

Many believe that traditional Christianity is thoroughly discredited for modern man. Some believe classical Christianity can be salvaged if Chalcedon is seen in the light of the basic Christian motif of Agape, allowing the creed to portray a real Person, who in turn implies a real community, thus giving us true man and true community findable only through right relation to God. Others, again, believe that we have to begin with the few scattered historic facts we have and build upon them some faith more nearly in the spirit and power of the historic Jesus and of the original Christian community. In this book, however, we have an example of a scholar who believes that the Bible, history, and systematic theology come together naturally in Christology to show us truth and salvation for a new and a more effective day. My heart is with the author in his great undertaking even though my mind refuses to bow to the constructed witness of synoptic unity.

If the first part of the volume were the main contribution, I should not be writing this Foreword. The two remaining sections, however, are important in approach. A strong thinker, good scholar, and faithful believer proposes Christology in terms of Christ as the fulfilling relation between God and man. The two nature theory is indispensable to any adequate rendering of the Christian doctrine of incarnation. But most theories are based on substance philosophy. Dr. Singh stresses instead the dynamic, active unity of God and man in one genuine personality. The book is worth publishing for this approach alone. It is not reduced to organismic philosophy and still a good deal of the truth of the organic relationship is there.

Dr. Pittenger's great work, *The Word Incarnate*, suffered from swallowing a bit uncritically organismic philosophy to the detriment of postorganismic thinking. In Singh's work the personal nature of the incarnation both in history and in eternity has more scope. In neither book is the full humanity accepted except in vigorous affirmation. There is no clear pointing to how God in Christ became sin for our sake to give us his own righteousness by overcoming in man the power of sin. As a matter of fact both books need more development not

only of humanity in Christ but also of the way God works to
atone the world's sin in the life, death, and resurrection of Jesus
Christ.

There can be no question, however, that Dr. Singh's book
raises the central issue. He is, to be sure, confessionally ardent
about the uniqueness of Jesus Christ, but as in the case of the
resurrection, he never becomes clear on uniqueness in relation
to the two natures in Christ and the two natures in the believer. Relational uniqueness can mean historic and positional
primacy and irreversibility. Can Christ be unique beyond such
an affirmation without denying, at least eschatologically, either
the humanity of Jesus or the presence of the Second Person of
the Trinity in the believer — "unless ye have the Spirit of
Christ, ye are none of his"? The author has raised the basic
questions for the reader to wrestle with and grow in grace and
understanding, for like the long list of Christological interpreters Singh refuses to draw back the veil of the actual union in
Christ.

The final section deals with the main threat to the Christian
faith in our day. The supernatural, personalistic, classical Christian faith is now being undermined by an ultimately nondualistic, impersonal, or transpersonal faith. The winds are
blowing gale-strong out of the Orient. Our seminary students
prate, sometimes innocently, about "the transcendence of sub-
ject-object relations." Ministers are reading everywhere theol-
ogies that call a personal God and real life everlasting pre-
liminary, symbolic doctrines until the fuller meaning of true
ontology is understood and accepted. The main fight, make
no mistake, is between the Christian faith in its inner classical
meaning and the new Orientalized versions whether they come
via Neoplatonism or in modern forms. The main advocates will
wear Christian garb and profess to be Christian interpreters.

Dr. Singh raises the question of the personal nature of the
Christian faith in its most telling modern setting: the confrontation with Hinduism in two of its greatest exponents, the classical thinker, Śankara, and the modern prophet, Radhakrishnan.

As I read this conflict in the light of the author's discussion of the implications of Christology I was intrigued by it and seized by its critical importance. The sophisticated and informed reader will recognize thought for thought the most popular " Christian " theology of our day.

Even I, after considerable study of Hinduism, began to see many new issues and became fascinated by what the modern Hindus are doing to prepare for a world-wide faith. Never before have I been more favorably disposed to the Hindu faith as presented by Radhakrishnan, even when reading him directly, because of his having struggled with the Christian presuppositions. The faith of the theologians who present the same faith under Christian symbols also took on new attraction. We shall come up against this attraction increasingly.

If the classical Christian faith is to weather the world-wide climate and come out a truly universal message, it must listen long and well to other living voices of faith. Dr. Singh has done just this and come out with a ringing, even gripping, confession of the Christian faith with its personal, prophetic categories. Since I believe that we Christians have to face this conflict from now on and since I know that Surjit Singh has given us deep and telling insights from the radically Christian perspective, how can I help wanting to introduce this book to the Christian world? Nor must or will it stop there. In this work modern man can confront himself and his basic choice of ultimates. Let the light shine.

NELS F. S. FERRÉ
Abbot Professor of Christian Theology
Andover Newton Theological School
Newton Centre, Massachusetts

PREFACE

I AM GLAD to know that Dr. Ferré has been recommending
the study of my Christological views to his students and
friends. I am all the more glad that he has found it possible to
write a foreword to my book. But I am particularly glad that
he has initiated a theological conversation on the theme of the
book.

Dr. Ferré is correct in stating that the book is written from
a postcritical perspective. He identifies himself as one " still
caught in the critical tradition of unregenerate scholarship."
When, therefore, he approaches my postcritical position from
his own, he often reads into it precritical connotations. He vin-
dicates "unregenerate scholarship" uncritically because he
blurs the critical distinction between the precritical and the
postcritical.

This is the main reason he lumps together Fundamentalist and
ecumenical scholarship, equates postcriticism with resurgent
conservatism, postcritical with precritical hermeneutics, and
identifies Singh with Athanasius — not that I mind the company.
To illustrate his point he states, among other things, that I run
roughshod over clear manuscript evidence in attributing to
Jesus, and not to the plural believers, the being born not of
blood, flesh, or man, but of the will of God. Let the reader examine the context and he will find that I am simply stating the
position of C. F. Burney and William Temple. In the same vein
he accuses me of creating a "rhapsody of orthodoxy" on the

17

Son of Man, whereas the book will amply show that the right
and the left of New Testament scholarship converge in asserting
that the solution of the Son of Man problem is well within
sight.

Dr. Ferré further asserts that I am more orthodox than the
New Testament. According to him, I read back into the New
Testament the later doctrinal unity of the ecumenical councils
and thereby fall prey to a precritical Biblicism. I must admit
that this is a constant danger when we try to approach the
New Testament from the motifs of Agape, New Being, existence, eschatology, or resurrection. But the risk has to be
taken. I do not claim that there is any schematic unity in the
New Testament, although it would be uncritical to deny some
theologizing tendency. What I do assert is that there is a unitary
Person to whom many have borne witness. The unity of the
Person of Jesus Christ is primary and the unity of the manifold
witness is derivative. This derived unity becomes increasingly
self-conscious and schematic in the formulations of church
councils such as Chalcedon.

Dr. Ferré also accepts the division of thinkers into the
Pythagoreans, who accept the a priori of principle or faith, and
the Ionians, who appeal to fact and inquiry. He makes me out
a Pythagorean and himself Pythagorean-Ionian. He, however,
perceptively remarks that my Christology is based not on substance philosophy but upon *relation*. And it is not substance but
relation that makes the interplay of deduction and induction
possible. It is relation that unites faith and fact. It is this phenomenon which creates the postcritical perspective.

I am indeed deeply appreciative of Dr. Ferré's thoughtful
and generous foreword. The conversation is open to the reader.

Many esoteric movements have arisen on the fringes of organ-
ized religion in America. Some such as Christian Science, the
Theosophical Society, and the Vedanta Society are well known.
But there are many others calling themselves "metaphysical"

in one sense or another. In addition there are countless small groups of gnostic orientation spread throughout the country having some special areas of concentration such as California.

These movements attract people who are dissatisfied with organized religion and especially in revolt against institutional Christianity. Another common feature shared by these movements and sects is a nondualistic philosophy largely derived from India. Even the Zen Buddhism that has come to this country through Japan has deep roots in the philosophical thought of India and cannot be fully understood without that background.

This advaitic, or nondualistic, philosophy is largely ahistorical, apersonal, and atemporal. The values at stake are of personality, of history, and of time. Our concern is not so much to save the "organizedness" of institutional Christianity as to indicate a way to safeguard the reality of personality, human and divine, of history, of time, and of the world. This can best be done by recapturing afresh the New Testament significance of the person and work of Jesus Christ. It is the person and work of Jesus Christ that raises most acutely the question of the reality of God, of man, and of the world.

The first three chapters are devoted to this investigation. The results of this investigation, coupled with the Christian experience of the writer, form the basis of Chapter IV. In that chapter an attempt has been made to reconstruct the outlines of an adequate Christology. The course followed is to emphasize the unity of the Person of Jesus Christ rather than the divine and human sides. He is conceived as the Relation — the God-Man.

In Chapter V a point of contact and departure is sought. It is the philosophy of Dr. S. Radhakrishnan. He is the best-known Indian idealistic philosopher. He has a highly attractive modernized version of nondualistic philosophy. It is his type of philosophy which consciously or unconsciously lies behind most of the esoteric sectarian movements. A concise critical account of his philosophy is presented. In this way Christian thought and experience is related to nondualistic philosophy.

This interrelation of two viewpoints, however, is dealt with actually in Chapter VI. There the personal existence of God and
man is re-established. The thought of Radhakrishnan in the last
resort does away with these two. It is only on the basis of Jesus
Christ that such a rehabilitation can take place. The last chapter gathers up all the underlying threads and endeavors to present, within a limited scope, a philosophy of personality.

For an adequate understanding of the last chapter, and, for
that matter, of the whole book, a biographical note may be
added. The writer, coming from an idealistic background, had
at a certain stage of his life a terrible experience of meaninglessness. This experience lasted in one form or another for some
years. Finally this experience of nothingness was conquered.
This happened through Jesus Christ as the God-Man — one with
man as a man but at the same time carrying man beyond into
the sphere of meaning and creative living. He created in the
inner depths of the writer a deep sense of communion with the
Personal Presence, giving him thereby a sense of meaning,
fulfillment, and creative growth. It is thus the conviction of the
writer that personality is created in relation — in relation between the human I and the divine Thou. This is the basic fact.

In Jesus Christ humanity has reached its full measure of manhood. With the conquest of anxiety — that primary condition
of our being from which arises all sin — in the life of Jesus
Christ reconciliation has taken place between God and man.
Now the intention of God for man can be realized in individual
human beings and in human history at large. Not only that,
but even the world of nature can be redeemed. Jesus Christ is
the express image of the character of God. In the historical
koinōnia the disciples' fellowship with their master created in
them a sense of personal worth and destiny. They became per-
sonalities — the children of God. Moreover, they received a
vocation from this fellowship, and that is to awaken in men
and women everywhere a high sense of personal destiny which
God in his infinite mercy has bestowed upon them. Thus the
fullness of the measure of the stature of the Son of God is

realized through reconciliation with God and then with man and the world. This inner reconciliation results in a coherent outlook by which man no more sees his life piecemeal but as a related whole. This unity of inner and outer life is first achieved in the historical life of Jesus Christ. Then upon whoever enters into the relationship of love and trust with him, he confers the power and right to bear the image of God — to become a personality in the true sense of the term. In Christ the primary relation is of person to person, and all other relations, of man and woman, of husband and wife, of parent and child, etc., follow after it. In the order of importance the fundamental relation is *personal* and not sexual, parental, or sociocultural. The primacy of the person-to-person relation does not render it abstract. On the contrary this relation is at once grounded in the divine-human dimension and the sociocultural dimension. The social dimension is no doubt indispensable, but it is also more obvious than the other. The divine-human dimension is hidden and often considered dispensable, but it provides more securely the relational freedom which is the birthplace of personality. Thus personality is created and achieved in relation — relation between God and man through Jesus Christ.

SURJIT SINGH

San Anselmo, California

I

LIGHT ON CHRISTIAN ORIGINS

SCHOLARLY OPINION has swung back and forth between whether Christianity is of Hebrew or of Greek origin. Advocates of one view have tried to explain the other away. The last swing of the pendulum of opinion was in favor of the Jewish origin. The presupposition of this view was that the Hellenistic element was foreign and imported from outside Palestine. Along with this went the idea that New Testament writings such as the Fourth Gospel, which displayed Hellenistic influences, were of late origin.

This schematism of the Jewish and Gentile background of the New Testament has been steadily dissolving under the recognition that both elements were constituent parts of an original situation, and that the Hellenistic element was internal to Palestine. Behind the phenomenon of Jewish-Hellenistic Christianity was present, of course, Hellenistic Judaism, an esoteric form of orthodox Judaism. T. W. Manson [1] in his *The Servant-Messiah* ventures to suggest, and Cullmann [2] conditionally agrees, that originally the word " pharisee " simply meant " Persian," and then the name stuck. The Pharisees were the upholders of tradition, but this tradition was living and growing. It was open to fresh ideas. Manson is not anxious to decide the question whether the characteristic doctrines of the Pharisees were derived from Persia or developed under Persian influence. The fact is that they constitute the background in the earliest Christian theology. Compared to the Pharisees and the Sadducees, the Essenes are the least important.

The Dead Sea scrolls found in the different caves of Wâdī Qumrân (and Wâdī Muraba'ât) have shed much light on the question of Christian origins. In the first flush of discovery there was a wild wave of journalistic sensationalism implying that the whole Christian movement in origin and substance had been reduced to insignificant proportions. André Dupont-Sommer asserted that Jesus was a mere reincarnation of the Teacher of Righteousness. Edmund Wilson claimed that the seat of the Qumrân community was the real birthplace of Christianity. As such it was a product of social evolution, an incident in history and not in any sense of divine origin. John Allegro went farther and proclaimed that the Qumrân community anticipated and approximated Christianity much more closely: the Teacher of Righteousness had been crucified and was expected by his followers to rise from the dead and return as messiah and judge at the end of the world. Allegro later withdrew these statements as being based on inference rather than on evidence.

After the uproar of extravagant claims had settled down, the picture of the relationship between the Dead Sea scrolls and the New Testament began to fall into proper focus. The statement of Millar Burrows: "Everything that is important in the last two or three centuries before Christ and in the first century A.D. is important also for Christianity. By enriching our understanding of Judaism in the period in which Christianity arose, the Dead Sea scrolls have given us material for a better understanding of the New Testament and early Christianity. It has even been said that the discoveries will revolutionize New Testament scholarship. This may perhaps cause some alarm. There is no danger, however, that our understanding of the New Testament will be so revolutionized by the Dead Sea scrolls as to require a revision of any basic article of Christian faith. All scholars who have worked on the texts will agree that this has not happened and will not happen," [3] may on the whole be considered representative of New Testament scholarship. Professor Burrows reconsidered this statement in the light of fresh objections and reconfirmed it. [4]

This does not mean that the seriousness of the statements that Christianity is an "episode" of history and that the Teacher of Righteousness was crucified, will rise from the dead, and will return as messiah and judge, is lightly treated. Both Krister Stendahl and Oscar Cullmann in their respective essays in *The Scrolls and the New Testament,* take these objections seriously and answer them effectively. Stendahl shows there is no inherent contradiction between an episode of history and divine revelation. And along with Cullmann he makes the point that in spite of instructive similarities the most crucial difference is constituted by the fact that the crucified Teacher of Righteousness will rise, whereas the crucified Jesus has already risen from the dead. It is Jesus crucified and risen that makes the difference. Stendahl says, "The relative difference in anticipation led to what appears to us an absolute difference in ideas." Cullmann says: "Unavoidably, the Teacher of Righteousness has drawn attention to himself and raised the possibility of drawing parallels with Christianity. In spite, however, of all the historical and theological lines of contact, the difference remains in the Person, teaching, and work of Jesus, and in the role played by his death in the theological thinking of the early church." Cullmann goes on to remark that this difference leads to another which is the coming of the Holy Spirit in the church. By contrast the Qumrân community was an organization.

The discovery of the Gnostic library at Nag-Hammadi in Upper Egypt, about the same time as the Qumrân texts, throws additional light on the origin of Christianity. C. H. Dodd in his book *The Bible and the Greeks* undertook to study the relation between the Hermetica and Hellenistic Judaism in the light of the Septuagint. He came to the conclusion that the influence of Gentile thought on Judaism is reciprocal and not one-sided. "It has been customary of late to emphasize the influence of Gentile thought upon Judaism, and that influence was unquestionably enormous. But it would not be safe to assume that where Hellenistic Judaism shows parallels with non-Jewish thought, the debt lies always and wholly upon one side." [5]

Robert M. Grant, after listing the various explanations of the origin of Gnosticism such as Hellenistic philosophy, Oriental religion, Christianity, and heterodox Judaism, defends the position that Gnosticism came into existence largely because of the failure of Jewish apocalyptic-eschatological hopes consequent upon the downfall of Jerusalem.[6] Hans Jonas, while welcoming the evidence of descent from Judaism as a needful correction along with other contributory elements, remarks, "Indeed, so far as traceable pedigrees of elements go, all investigations of detail over the last half century have proved divergent rather than convergent, and leave us with a portrait of Gnosticism in which the absence of a unifying character seems to be the salient feature." [7]

This all goes to show that Gnosticism was a complex phenomenon in a varied environment. For our purposes it is certain that prior to Hellenistic Christianity there was Hellenistic Judaism, and that there is an internal and integral relationship between the two. Scholars accept in principle the common identity of the Essenes and the Qumrân community. Whether this identity is absolute or relative is an open question. And it is probably here that the above-quoted opinion of T. W. Manson may have a degree of relevance. The question also naturally arises about John the Baptist and his followers. Cullmann speculates that there could be a connection between Jesus and the Qumrân community through John the Baptist. This might explain the phenomenon of similarities, but what about the decisive differences? In defense Cullmann advances his principle of interpretation that " one movement may very well grow out of another and still stand in opposition to it." [8]

THE HELLENISTS OF THE ACTS

Increasing attention is being devoted by New Testament scholars to the Hellenists of the book of The Acts in the belief that they are a very significant clue to the understanding of the

origin and expansion of Christianity. They were members of
the original Palestinian Christian community. They are called
Hellenists in contradistinction to the "Hebrews" for lack of a
better term. They are distinguished not by their language but
by their Greek manner of living.[9] There were two types of emphasis in early Christianity. While both were Christian, one
oriented the new faith toward Judaism and the other tried to
go beyond it. The latter can be characterized Hellenists and
the former Hebrews. Whereas this distinction is valid, no material advantage is gained by dividing them geographically between Samaria and Jerusalem as E. Lohmeyer tried to do. It is
clear that in the early phase of the Christian movement the
Hebrews were in the ascendancy; but later the Hellenists came
into full control.

It is evident from Acts, chs. 6 to 8, that the "seven men of
good repute" picked to serve at tables did much more than
that. In fact, they enjoyed a status among the Hellenists com-
parable to what the apostles had among the Hebrews. There
are two points of dispute between the Hellenists and the Jews
(and Christians of Jewish orientation): the Law and the Temple. According to Stephen's speech in Acts, ch. 7, Jesus Christ
has superseded both the Law and the Temple. The Jews as a
consequence stoned him to death and persecuted the other
Hellenists; but the apostles remained unharmed at Jerusalem.
We learn from Acts 8:4-5 that these persecuted and scattered
Hellenists went about preaching the Word and that Philip
went to a city of Samaria and proclaimed the name of Christ.

A study of Luke 9:51 f.; Luke 10:30 f.; and Luke 17:11 f.
shows that the Third Evangelist is very much interested in the
contacts of Jesus with Samaria.[10] There is probably here a
point of affinity between Luke and the Fourth Gospel. The
Fourth Evangelist in the fourth chapter of his Gospel makes
the case that Jesus himself is the source of the missionary activity in Samaria and that the Hellenists of The Acts are the
original initiators of the Christian movement because these are
the "others" (John 4:38) who had labored before the apostles

Peter and John arrived on the scene. This is all according to the purpose of Jesus, and the Hellenists are true to his intention. The Evangelist is very sympathetic to the Hellenists and may have had a close relationship to them.

We do not know very much about these Hellenists. About their beliefs and ideas the only reasonably full account we possess is in Stephen's discourse recorded in Acts, ch. 7. Judging from the general outline of Stephen's thought, it becomes highly probable that they had a clearer grasp of the mission and message of Jesus than the Jews had. Stephen's unique employment of the phrase " Son of Man " is in itself of decisive importance in this context. This " more-than-Jewish-Messianic " grasp, as William Manson calls it, is further illustrated when the dying martyr gazing at heaven sees " the glory of God " and Jesus standing at the right hand of God, and says, " Behold, I see the heavens opened, and the Son of man standing at the right hand of God."

The Eschatology of the Hellenists

William Manson, while interpreting the thought of the epistle to the Hebrews in the light of the Stephen tradition, makes the following comment on the above-mentioned vision. " Stephen's direction of mind towards the Ultimate Event in the revelation of God in Christ appears here with extraordinary vividness, and it is impossible not to ask whether in this direction of mind, ordinarily called eschatology, we have not the true key to his characteristic work and witness and to much else that follows in the history of the world-mission of Christianity." [11] In further elaboration W. Manson develops the thought that all the apostles and their followers were eschatologists, but they expected Jesus to come *back* to them. Whereas Stephen, who had seen the Son of Man arrive in the presence of God and receive from him dominion over the whole world, believed in leaving the Temple, the Law, and the past behind and *going out* to meet the Son of Man. He anticipates the Son of Man by proclaiming him to the whole world which had already become his inheritance.

Luke, the historian, places the young man Saul, who later became Paul, at the scene of Stephen's martyrdom.[12] And it becomes increasingly certain that lines of connection can be traced from these Palestinian Hellenist Christians to the Synoptics, to Paul, to John, and to the epistle to the Hebrews.

Wrede's thoroughgoing skepticism and Schweitzer's thoroughgoing eschatology destroyed the liberal picture of Jesus by showing that the Marcan text has no connecting links between the pericopes of its narrative. In other words, there is a complete lack of connection in the text of Mark. Both agree that there is a way of making sense out of this chaos. There is a dogmatic element present in the description of the life of Jesus which has no connection with the outward course of that life. This dogmatic element is the Messianic secret of Jesus. According to Wrede, Jesus was not aware of his being the Messiah, nor is it the work of Mark. The ascription of Messiahship is post-resurrection and is the work of the Christian community.

Schweitzer departs from Wrede in saying that Jesus was aware of his being the Messiah but he kept it a secret. He divulged it to the disciples at Caesarea Philippi and it is this secret which Judas sold to the priests. And furthermore, the Messianic secret is only a part of the mystery of the Kingdom of God. This idea of the Kingdom can be understood only against the environment which was saturated by the Jewish apocalyptic and eschatological hopes. According to Schweitzer, Jesus can be understood only against this background. "Eschatology is simply 'dogmatic history' — history as moulded by theological beliefs — which breaks in upon the natural course of history and abrogates it."[13]

By the exegesis of Matt. 10:23, Schweitzer shows that Jesus expected the dawn of the Kingdom, which is identical with the parousia of the Son of Man, before the disciples were able to return from their journey through the towns of Israel. The disciples returned, but the prediction did not come about. The actual course of events negated the dogmatic history upon which Jesus based his action. "That was for Jesus, who lived wholly in the dogmatic history, the first 'historical' occurrence, the central event which closed the former period of his activity and gave the new period a new character." [14] Consistent, therefore, with his dogmatic conviction Jesus makes the Messianic entry into Jerusalem in order to force the coming of the Kingdom of God through his suffering and crucifixion. His ethics is interim ethics, for when the Kingdom comes there will be no need of ethics. Schweitzer believes profoundly that only a consistent and thoroughgoing eschatology can explain the life of Jesus in the Marcan text. In fact, the whole history of dogma should be expounded in this way, whereas the contrary and dominant practice is based on the abandonment of eschatology.

Schweitzer complains that "the whole history of Christianity down to the present day, that is to say, the real inner history of it, is based on the delay of the parousia, the nonoccurence of the parousia, the abandonment of eschatology, the progress and completion of 'de-eschatologizing' of religion which has been connected therewith." [15] Martin Werner has brilliantly defended this elaborate thesis of Schweitzer in his book *The Formation of Christian Dogma.*

The great merit of Schweitzer's work is that he has made the discussion of eschatology indispensable for Biblical and theological thought. If the liberal Jesus did not survive the attack of consistent eschatology, it is equally hard to find where the eschatological Jesus is. Schweitzer builds too heavily on the exegesis of Matthew, particularly Matt. 10:23. He fails to take into account the synoptic evidence that the Kingdom was in a way already present in the ministry of Jesus, that his ethics was much more serious than a mere *ad hoc* arrangement. It is no wonder that C. H. Dodd seizes upon these weaknesses to break through Schweitzer's highly elaborate thesis.

C. H. Dodd in *The Apostolic Preaching* develops the point of view of realized eschatology over against consistent eschatology. By quoting representative propositions from all parts of the New Testament he makes the point that, "for the New

Testament writers in general, the *eschaton* has entered history; the hidden rule of God has been revealed; the age to come has come. The gospel of primitive Christianity is a gospel of realized eschatology."[16] Dodd is equally emphatic about the ethics of Jesus. He takes into full account the evidence of the Synoptics, of Paul, and of John. In particular about the Gospel of Matthew he says, "It combines *kērygma* with *didachē*, and if we regard the book as a whole, the element of *didachē* predominates."[17] This is in direct contrast to Schweitzer's theory of interim ethics. In further elaboration of the arguments concerning ethics Dodd argues that Jesus was not deluded about the end of the world, but expected history to continue after his departure. He therefore prepared his disciples for the times of trouble and gave them guidance how to act and meet the challenge of such times. Accordingly, the ethics of the Sermon on the Mount is "too universal" and "too permanent" to be merely designated as "interim ethics," applicable to a very short period before the end of the world.[18]

In a situation of reaction Dodd is so preoccupied with the challenge of Schweitzer that his own, otherwise wholesome emphasis on realized eschatology, becomes one-sided. Although he is aware of the fact of the Second Coming and the Last Judgment,[19] this is not enough to mitigate the dominant emphasis on realized eschatology. It is only in his later writings that he corrects his earlier overemphasis perhaps in recognition of the fact that it has successfully performed its function. Commenting on the statement that Jesus made before the high priest, "You shall see the Son of Man seated at the right hand of the Almighty." Dodd makes a comprehensive statement representative of his present position. "I hesitate," he says, "even to press any single saying, where all are so enigmatic; but surely the total impression is that the forecasts of a coming of Christ in history (fulfilled in his resurrection) are balanced by forecasts of a coming beyond history: definitely, I say, *beyond* history, and not as a further event *in* history, not even the last event."[20] In order to avoid any further misunderstanding of "realized eschatology" he accepts its emendation as "inaugurated eschatology." [21]

Bultmann advances a position quite different from that of Schweitzer and of Dodd. He seems to agree with Schweitzer that the message of Jesus can best be understood against the background of Jewish apocalyptic thought, but regards all futuristic reference to the end of the world as pure myth and radically demythologizes it. He eliminates all temporal reference to the future in the cosmic physical sense of this term.

He seems to agree with Dodd that the Kingdom of God is in some way present in historical time, but then immediately dehistorizes history and detemporalizes time. The result is quite radical because time in its historical and cosmic dimensions is completely detached from the reign of God and therefore this concept becomes eschatological. The reign of God is the dominant concept of the message of Jesus. According to Bultmann the preaching of Jesus can be summarized in the saying, "The time is fulfilled, and the reign of God is at hand" (Mark 1:15). The sign of the drawing and breaking in of the reign of God is Jesus himself. "Basically, therefore," asserts Bultmann, "*he in his own person is the ' sign of the time.'* Yet the historical Jesus of the Synoptics does not, like the Johannine Jesus, summon men to acknowledge or 'believe in' his person. He does not proclaim himself as the Messiah, i.e., the King of the time of salvation, but he points ahead to the Son of Man as another than himself." [22] Jesus only signifies the demand for decision in favor of or against God. He calls for decision because now is the time for decision, and God desires radical obedience from the whole man.

This means that Jesus' eschatological message and his ethical message form a unity. The aim of this message is not to form character or mold society but to demand decision, and this is what salvation means. "The reign of God, demanding of man decision for God against every earthly tie, is the salvation to come. Hence, only he is ready for this salvation who in the concrete moment decides for that demand of God which confronts him in the person of his neighbor." [23] The essential content, therefore, of the eschatological message of Jesus is not that the end of the world is at hand, but rather, the idea of God and of human existence which it contains.

The confrontation of God and man is an eschatological occurrence and takes place in the eschatological now. And when cosmic and historical time is abstracted from the meaning of "now," it turns out to be ontological existence as understood in the Husserl-Heidegger tradition. In Bultmann's version when God and man are "dehistorized," where history means the affairs of nations, they are at once radically "historized" in a different sense of history that means eschatologized history. This is the theological equivalent of Heidegger's ontological assertion. At this critical point I shall let Bultmann speak for himself:

"For Jesus, however, man is desecularized by God's direct pronouncement to him, which tears him out of all security of any kind and places him at the brink of the end. And God is 'desecularized' by understanding His dealing eschatologically: He lifts man out of his worldly ties and places him directly before His own eyes. Hence, the 'de-historization' or 'de-secularization' both of God and of man is to be understood as a paradox (*dialektisch*): precisely that God, who stands aloof from the history of nations, meets each man in his own little history, his everyday life with its daily gift and demand; dehistorized man (i.e., naked of his supposed security within his historical group) is guided into his concrete encounter with his neighbor, in which he finds his true history." [24]

The kerygma in the hands of Bultmann has so "dehistorized" the New Testament that his disciples in Europe and America are raising the question of the historical Jesus in a new way. Indications of this are found in Günther Bornkamm's *Jesus von Nazareth* and James Robinson's *A New Quest of the Historical Jesus*. This is done not by repudiating Bultmann's estimate of the sources, but rather by availing themselves of a new view of history and self as found in Dilthey and existentialism. In other words, the new quest is to be pursued through a theology of history. The movement is suggestive, but what the outcome will be remains to be seen. Even Bultmann himself points in this direction in a significant way.

In his *Promise and Fulfillment,* W. G. Kümmel undertakes a comprehensive examination of "consistent," "realized," and "atemporal" eschatologies. He interrogates the sources and through skillful exegesis tries to show that these eschatologies are untenable. He comes to the conclusion that "the true meaning of Jesus' eschatological message is to be found in its reference to God's action in Jesus himself, that the essential content of Jesus' preaching about the Kingdom of God is the news of the divine authority of Jesus, who appeared on earth and is awaited in the last days as the one who effects the divine purpose of mercy." [25] It is clear, as we have shown above, that Dodd has corrected his one-sidedness; but unfortunately Kümmel has not taken notice of it. After examining different interpretations of eschatology, we are led to the confirmation that Stephen and his group had a clear and firm grasp of the life and purpose of Jesus.

Wrede and Schweitzer had already questioned the firmness of Mark's outline. Their point was that there was no inner connection, but that a dogmatic interest either on the part of the Christian community or of Mark himself joined together the different isolated pericopes. It was, however, K. L. Schmidt who thoroughly investigated this question in his *Der Rahmen der Geschichte Jesus.* Schmidt's conclusion was that in spite of a few connected narrative passages the framework of Mark is on the whole purely artificial. This conclusion is strengthened by the later form-critical investigations, especially of a radical and skeptical variety. Many scholars are therefore led to believe that there is no synoptic outline of any credibility. The net gain from this type of investigation is that a simple return to a preform-critical position is completely barred. But since form criticism (literally form history) is a literary method and not a historical method, the above-mentioned extreme position is untenable and also discloses the limitations of form criticism. It seems the judgment of C. H. Dodd that " it is hazardous to argue from the precise sequence of the narrative in detail; yet there is good reason to believe that in broad lines the Marcan order does represent a genuine succession of events, within which movement and development can be traced," [26] is representative of the broad stream of New Testament scholarship.

ARAMAIC ORIGINS

Much progress has been made in the Aramaic origins of the Gospels and of The Acts. Dalman, Burney, and Torrey assumed that the Targums of Onkelos and Jonathan were representative of the language of Jesus. Burney believed that there was an Aramaic original lying behind the Fourth Gospel, and Torrey thought that all our Gospels were Greek translations from original Aramaic sources. Difficulties in the Greek text can be explained through mistranslation of the Aramaic. By correcting mistranslations they try to solve the " Aramaic problem."

Schulthess, Wensinck, Kahle, and Black break new ground. They reject the thesis that the Aramaic of the Targums of Onkelos and Jonathan is closer to the language of Jesus because it is heavily Hebraized and shows Babylonian influences. Alternatively they maintain that the Aramaic of the recently discovered manuscripts in the Genizah or lumber room of a synagogue in old Cairo gives us an authentic clue to the Aramaic spoken by Jesus.

Matthew Black lays down three conditions for the validity of the mistranslation thesis of Burney and particularly of Torrey. The mistranslation must be credible, the conjectured Aramaic must be possible, and it must have inherent probability in its Aramaic context.[27] His general conclusion as stated in his *An Aramaic Approach to the Gospels and Acts* is that an Aramaic sayings-source of tradition lies behind the Synoptic Gospels; but whether that source was written or oral cannot be decided from the existing state of the evidence.[28]

THE DIVINITY OF JESUS CHRIST

THE NEW TESTAMENT WRITERS

THE CHRISTIAN SCRIPTURES make extraordinary statements about Jesus Christ. These statements are nowhere defended by a reasoned and sustained argument. The writers of the New Testament seem to have been governed by motives other than the scientifically objective in the strictly scientific sense of the term. Therefore they do not give a descriptive analysis of the life of Jesus Christ but instead write as if their destiny gained its meaning and direction from him. When they wrote and preached to others their burden was the same.

This, of course, does not mean that the picture of Jesus Christ as presented in the Gospels is simply the creation of their fancy and wishful thinking. It has been proved beyond doubt by historical research that they are presenting a person with whom they had had actual contact in time and space. On the other hand, in this presentation of theirs they are giving us a sound view of history, because when they are dealing with it they are involved in it and do not occupy a balcony seat above the march of historical events. As a matter of fact, one of their company says that if everything Jesus said and did was recorded, volumes could be written. This clearly shows that their interest was not merely descriptive but selective — selective because it involved the coming of God and the salvation of man. It was of momentous importance because a vital issue was at stake. It was a question of life and death.

The writers of the New Testament were not trained theologians or metaphysicians; they were preachers and pastors who presented Jesus Christ as Savior and Lord to their churches and to the people who came under their influence.

THE QUESTION OF THE DIVINITY

The question of the divinity or deity of Jesus Christ arose out of the experience of salvation. The preachers and those who accepted the gospel of the preachers believed Christ to be their Savior. The question naturally arose, What relation does Jesus Christ bear to God? This question is found, but not in any conscious form, in the later strata of New Testament writings. Earlier than that we have no reason to doubt that those who believed Jesus Christ to be the Savior also believed in his divinity. These earlier strata of New Testament writings (one or two passages excepted) do not show any questioning on the part of the believers, nor do the writers show that such a question was raised from outside. It is mainly in the Fourth Gospel that we find such an awareness on the part of the writer. The question was raised most vigorously in the second, third, fourth, and fifth centuries, when it was thoroughly discussed, and the church finally adopted a Christological formula at the Council of Chalcedon with a view to guarding against all possible heresies. The church mainly defined its position in sets of negatives.

THE PAULINE WRITINGS

It is pretty well agreed among New Testament scholars that Paul nowhere uses the word "God" for Christ. It appears to be done only in Rom. 9:5, but the exegesis and the punctuation of the verse are so dubious that it is hard to make out a case from it. The confusion on this issue is clearly shown by two leading commentaries. Sanday and Headlam, while commenting on the controversial part of v. 5, adopt one alternative and say: "St. Paul's phraseology is never fixed; he had no dogmatic reason against so using it. In these circumstances with some slight, but only slight, hesitation we adopt the first alternative and translate ' of whom is the Christ as concerning the flesh, who is over all, God blessed for ever. Amen.' " [1]

On the other hand C. H. Dodd translates the controversial part of the verse as " Blessed for evermore be the God who is over all! Amen! " and says: " Even though he [Paul] ascribes to Christ functions and dignities which are consistent with nothing else than deity, yet he pointedly avoids calling Him ' God.' " [2] The reason why Paul refrained from using the term " God" for Christ, whereas the theologians who followed him did not hesitate, lies in the fact that Paul was a Hebrew whereas they were Greek. This does not for a moment imply that there was any material difference between the faith of Paul and that of the theologians. It was a difference of background. Although Paul spoke Greek, his religious terms always bore Hebrew coloring. Moreover, *theos* is not the same as *elohim.*[3]

But Paul frequently uses the word " Lord " for Jesus. The confession of Lordship from the pagan background would mean that the converts were chosen to belong to the body of Christ. The acknowledgment of Christ's Lordship from the Hebrew standpoint would mean that God had conferred upon Christ his own name as the covenant God of Israel, to indicate that all divine activity for the salvation of men is henceforward concentrated in him.

From the Hebrew point of view Paul's use of the word " Lord " for Christ would be equal to calling him " God," for the reason that the Hebrews used the word *Adonai,* which means " Lord," for *Yahweh.*

It is clear that in Rom. 8:3 and Gal. 4:4, where the " sending " of the Son is mentioned, the pre-existence of Christ is implied. And II Cor. 8:9 shows that this " pre-existence was not merely ideal but real and actual." [4] Moreover, v. 6 in the famous second chapter of Philippians throws light on the nature of the pre-existent Christ. The Greek word *morphe* is differently translated. In KJV and RSV it is translated "form," but in Moffatt it is translated "nature." Both translations mean much the same — that the pre-existent had divine nature. The history of the interpretation of this verse is so checkered that it would not do us much good to enter into it at length — although in spite of various interpretations the meaning of the clause "who being in the form of God," or "though he was divine by nature," as referring to the divine nature of the pre-existent Christ, remains unimpaired. The same idea of the form or "image" is found in II Cor. 4:4 and Col. 1:15-16.

As early as I Cor. 8:6, Paul introduces an idea that does not recur in him very often. It is further elaborated in Col. 1:15-17. The thought presented here is that the Lord Christ Jesus is the Creator of us all and of the things in this world. Here Christ is presented in a cosmic setting as the Creator of all creatures. Since in all likelihood there was no tendency toward syncretism in the church in Corinth, it becomes increasingly difficult to explain how Paul came to this conception of Christ. Did he come to it through the Hebrew idea of wisdom as the organ in creation and providence or through the Greek *Logos*? This question is hard to answer.

Paul elaborates the above-mentioned thought in Col. 1:15-17. Here the relation of Christ to God as well as to creation is set forth. The relation to God is expressed by two phrases, that "he is the image of the invisible God," and "first-born before all creation." In our mind these two are correlatives; and by putting the first-born and the image, i.e., expressed representation, on a par we get the depth of the relation of Christ, or at this stage the Eternal Son of God, to God the Father. This simply shows that in the relation between God the Father and the Son there is no passage of time and no interstellar space. Nothing else is conceivable except distinction as such. There is no getting behind him or between him and God the Father. Here Paul has at least refuted one item of the speculative syncretism of Colossae by showing that Christ is not one of the creation standing only prior to the rest. He is the Creator and not one of the created.

Here we come to the second relation — Christ's relation to the world. The syncretistic scheme conceived of a hierarchy of intermediary agents of a creation that was made out of some pre-existent stuff called matter. That is how the *Logos* of Philo works. He is like an architect who thinks out his plans in his mind and then impresses them on matter whose existence is presupposed. According to Paul, all these intermediary agents of creation and the rest of creation are created by the "first-born of creation." He does not work on any external matter to realize the plan for creation, but he himself is the source of the being and existence of creation. Incidentally, Paul does not believe in that hierarchical scheme, or he would mention them all in their logical order. All that matters to him is that Christ is the source of the being of all the creation, including these intermediaries if any, and that the whole creation exists for him, and he is the one who holds it together.

This passage in Paul is indeed unique, because here alone he discusses such a view of Christ; elsewhere the emphasis is entirely religious and moral. But it should be clearly borne in mind that this presentation is not prompted primarily by metaphysical and cosmological reasons, but by religious and moral ones. The close affinity of this passage with the prologue of John has led many to doubt the Pauline authorship of this passage. E. F. Scott says: "The passage represents a loftier conception of Christ's Person than is found anywhere else in the writings of Paul, and comes very near to the view set forth in the prologue to the Fourth Gospel. For this reason some critics have questioned its authenticity."[5] The reasoning against Pauline authorship seems to be based on the view that Paul here identifies Christ with the Logos, although he does not use that special word, and that the development of the Logos conception in Christian circles was subsequent to Paul. We need not accept this, because we know that the church was aware of the existence of the Alexandrian philosophy. This is particularly shown through the example of Apollos, a fellow worker of Paul. Paul probably knew about the Alexandrian philosophy and its doctrine of wisdom and logos. He does not make use of this conception in his earlier writings, for a general and a special reason. For a general reason, because this doctrine was highly speculative. More especially, the church situations he was dealing with did not require it. But when, in the Colossian church, a situation arose that demanded such an explanation, Paul made full use of the conception, setting forth unambiguously the relation of Christ to the material cosmos and the powers thereof.

In certain passages in I Corinthians — chs. 3:23; 11:3; 15:28 — Paul is evidently trying to answer by anticipation certain problems that might endanger the future existence of the church to the point of losing its identity. In these passages the line of argument is different from the above-mentioned one, but it does not stand in substantial disagreement with it. What Paul was anticipating was probably the creation of some sort of Christ cult, in view of the fact that the church was surrounded by mystery cults in which local and particular gods were the sole focus of the worshipers' attention, and the cosmic Deity had receded more and more into the background. It is a fact that those early Christians at the time of Paul's writings were not indulging in any belief like this. A presentation like this by Paul is then attributed more to his foresight than to the actual situation in the church. Paul therefore very wisely leaves this suggestion that " the Christian worship was offered to God the Father and creator through Jesus Christ the Lord (8:6; etc.). The Synthesis might be mysterious, but it was there, at the heart of what Christians meant by God." [6]

THE EPISTLE TO THE HEBREWS

Anyone who approached this epistle with the hope of finding a reasoned account of the Person of Christ was indeed doomed to disappointment. As a matter of fact the writer employs various shades of thought to explicate his view of Christ; but it seems that almost deliberately he avoids every temptation to weave them into a closely knit fabric. This is most conspicuous when we look at his evaluation of the two natures in Christ. There is no doubt about the fact that he emphasizes equally both the divinity and the humanity of our Lord. In his description the two natures neither stand confused nor in any relationship of juxtaposition. But nowhere is to be found any evidence of a consistent relationship between the two. This insight is indeed of great value, and urges us to read and reread the epistle; but if the writer had adopted one view, the real value of his work would have been reduced to that of a mere reference book.

There are two main sensitively related trends of thought presented in the epistle — the Alexandrian and the Messianic. The writer of the epistle, who in all probability was an Alexandrian Jew of Hellenistic-Jewish background, was certainly familiar with Alexandrian philosophy. It is said about him that he may not have read Plato and other great philosophers of the Greek world; " but he was certainly familiar with the writings of the Jewish-Alexandrian philosophers, and knew the Wisdom of Solomon and also, probably, Philo." [7] It will be seen a little later whether or not he borrowed a suitable terminology or ideas from these thinkers. It now suffices to say that there is evidence of such a trend in the epistle. The illustration in a general way of this evidence is to be found in the fact that the writer cherishes a sacramental view of the universe of religious meaning, if not of the universe as such. According to him the Law and the things of the Law are a shadow, an outline and copies of the real things of heaven. This universe then stands in symbolic relation to the real one. This is brought out in Greek philosophy by Platonic " Ideas," which are real and self-subsistent, while the things of this world are merely their shadowy representations. Here then the relation of Alexandrian-Hellenistic thought to the present epistle becomes explicit.

The Messianic element is clearly brought out by such references as Heb. 2:8, 14; 4:8; 9:28; and 10:7. " Then I said, ' I am come — in the roll of the book it is written concerning me.' " (Heb. 10:7.) " So the Christ also, having been once offered in sacrifice in order that he might bear the sins of many, will appear a second time, separated from sin, to those who are eagerly expecting him, to make their salvation complete." (Heb. 9:28.) "The destruction of the power and authority of the devil through the death of Christ in 2:14 aligns the writer with the Messianic beliefs of the primitive church. The comparison in 4:8 of Joshua as one who gave a rest to Israel, the people of God, with Jesus who gave final rest, has the flavor of a national Messiah. And finally in 2:8-9, 'the coming One' is no longer the Son of David, but a pre-existent being — the heavenly man who, according to the mystical interpretation of the 8th Psalm, will finally put all things under his feet." [8]

But the writer of the Hebrews goes beyond this merely Messianic conception. He identifies this Messiah with "the Son of God" and thus makes Jesus (Christ) partake in the divine nature. He does it in such a way that the latter conception does not displace the former, but both are distinctly maintained. We shall enlarge on it when we come to the discussion of Jesus the High Priest as "the Son" or "the Son of God."

To anyone who reads this epistle in one sitting it becomes abundantly clear that the theme of the writer is Jesus as our high priest, and that the rest is subservient to this dominant idea. The author outlines two requirements of a high priest and then applies them to Jesus with a difference. The first requirement of a high priest is that he is "appointed" by God from among men (Heb. 5:1-2, 4, 5). This, of course, here means from the descendants of Aaron. The second requirement of a high priest is that he is "to act on behalf of men in matters relating to God, in order to offer both gifts and sin-offerings, and he must be one who is able to bear patiently with the ignorant and erring, because he himself also is beset with infirmity. And for this reason he is required to offer sin-offerings not only for the people but also for himself" (Heb. 5:1-3). The immediate consequence is that there have to be many high priests and that sin offerings have to be made continually and repeatedly. The reason for the first requirement is that the high priest has a limited span of life and is mortal (Heb. 7:23), and the second is that he is a sinner.

In applying these requirements to Jesus, the writer says concerning the first one: "And no one takes this honourable office upon himself, but only accepts it when called to it by God, as Aaron was. So Christ also did not claim for Himself the honour of being made High Priest, but was appointed to it by Him who said to Him, ' My Son art Thou: I have to-day become Thy Father ' (Ps. ii.7) " (Heb. 5:4-5). The difference here is that, whereas high priests were appointed from among the Levites, this high priest is not. He is of his own kind. The only analogy by which we can dimly understand it is of Melchizedek. " For God Himself addresses Him as a High Priest for ever, belonging to the order of Melchizedek." (Heb. 5:10.) This is a new order of priesthood with only one high priest, and a new covenant is established (Heb. 7:24).

According to the second requirement a high priest ministers to the "descendants of Abraham" and not to "angels" and not to stocks or to stones (Heb. 2:16). "And for this purpose it was necessary that in all respects He should be made to resemble His brothers, so that He might prove Himself a compassionate and faithful High Priest in things relating to God, in order to atone for the sins of the people. For inasmuch as He has Himself felt the pain of temptation and trial, He is also able to help those who are tempted and tried " (Heb. 2:17-18). After the author has very strongly emphasized the identification of this high priest with the needs of humanity, he goes on to point out a great difference between this high priest and every other high priest and, for that matter, every man. The uniqueness of this high priest lies in the fact that in spite of being tempted in every respect like every other man yet he did not sin (Heb. 4:15). This means that in atoning for sin he did not offer any sacrifice for himself. For if he was himself caught in the sin nexus and offered sacrifice for himself, he would have to do so from the foundation of the world ad infinitum. But when in actual fact he did not sin, it shows that he atones for others. Three consequences follow from this premise, and the author does not hesitate to state them. In the first place, his sacrifice is not repeatable, it is once for all. Secondly, he does not offer anything else but himself as sacrifice. And thirdly, this one who offers himself once for all is the Son of God, his " image," and " effulgence."

This brings us to the point where it is contended that the Jewish Alexandrian writer, in calling Jesus Christ, the Son of God, the " effulgence " of God's glory and the " image " of his Person, is drawing heavily on Philo and other sources in Jewish-Alexandrian philosophy. Critics are agreed that the terminology may be borrowed, but the thought and the idea expressed in the words is originally Christian. William Manson says that the writer is not interested in cosmology but in redemption. Moffatt, commenting on this controversial point, says: " The unique relation of Christ to God is one of the unborrowed truths of Christianity, but it is stated here in borrowed terms. The writer is using the metaphors which had been already applied in Alexandrian theology to Wisdom and the Logos." [9] Rawlinson says about the work of the Son of God in creation that it is taken over "more probably from St. Paul than Philo." [10] In the footnote on the same page he says that there are " close verbal parallels in the writings of Philo. . . . But it is improbable that he was directly dependent in a literary sense upon Philo." And E. F. Scott remarks that it may be supposed that " the Christian writer has taken over the Philonic conception of the Logos as 'the great high priest' and has applied it, with a few necessary modifications, to the work of Christ. But this conclusion ceases to be tenable when we have regard not merely to coincidences of language and metaphor, but to underlying ideas." [11]

The writer in identifying the high priest with the Son of God is really aiming at the determination of the nature of Christ and its pertinence to his work of redemption. That is why he uses such words as the " effulgence " of God's " glory " and the " express image " of his essence. According to Westcott

the first term "brings out the conception of the source of the
Son's Being, and of his unbroken connection with the Father,
as revealing to man the fullness of his attributes"; and the
second term "emphasizes the true personality of the Son as
offering in himself the perfect representation of the divine
essence of the Father." [12] According to him the two terms represent the Son as "co-essential" and "only-begotten." Moffatt,
however, says that the terms "effulgence" and "express image"
are intended to bring out the same idea. Just as the words
"glory" and "essence" also correspond with each other.[13] All
this implies that the Son is divine in nature and as such is as
high above the angels as God himself. According to the writer
of the Hebrews it is through the same Son that the creation
came into being, and he is the one who now sustains the entire
cosmos by the power of his word. The writer evidently does
not carry the same thought so explicitly throughout the entire
epistle, but it is certain that it is always in the back of his mind.
It is on the force and strength of such an identification of the
high priest with the Son and the presence of this thought in the
background of the total epistle that elicits from him a surpris-
ing statement regarding the function of Christ as the high
priest. In Heb. 9:14, he goes on to say that this high priest had
offered himself to God "through the eternal Spirit." Here we
find that the idea of the high priest which was present in
Judaism and also in Philo gains a unique distinction. It determines the nature of the high priest — the one who is offering
himself now is the one who had offered himself before God in
eternity. So to the writer of the epistle the life of the Son is
lived in all circumstances with unbroken continuity. He comes
to men from on high, he lives among them, is exalted far above
the angelic host, is heir to the universe, and sits on the right
hand of God Almighty. All this is in an unbroken series. It is
probably here that we find the important omission in the epistle
— the resurrection. Thus moves the thought of the writer of
this remarkable epistle.

THE SYNOPTICS

Peter's Confession

Scholars have regarded Peter's confession at Caesarea Philippi as the high-water mark of Gospel tradition. This point divides the ministry of Christ into two periods. It is true that some scholars have evaluated this confession as a creation of pious fancy, while others regard it as a fact of history. The confession of Peter, which is found in the Synoptics and also in John, asserts that Jesus is the Messiah, not, however, the messiah so longingly awaited by the Jews.[14] Wrede and Bultmann argue that Peter's confession is a pious legend because Jesus nowhere makes the claim of being a messiah and was not so regarded until after the resurrection. This faith of the early church was then transferred to the consciousness of Jesus; and Peter, since he was the leading disciple, was made the mouthpiece of this "Messianic Secret."[15] On the other hand, T. W. Manson and others argue that declaring himself as Messiah would not have helped matters, because to recognize the Messiah in Jesus does not require the organs of mere physical perception but of faith and spiritual discernment. Since this or the evidence for this was not there, Jesus did not freely talk about it, and whenever he did imply it he asked his disciples to be quiet. It is for that reason that Jesus in reply to Peter's confession says, "Blessed art thou, Simon Bar-Jonah: for flesh and blood hath not revealed it unto thee, but my Father which is in heaven" (Matt. 16:17). But when the evidence for such a faith was presented in the confession of Peter, "Thou art the Christ," (Mark 8:29), he did not disown Peter's calling him the Christ. As a matter of fact he went farther and explained to his disciples what kind of messiah he was. He was not a messiah of the popular apocalyptic expectations, but a messiah in line with the prophetic teaching and preaching. This may have disappointed Peter, but it does show that he did accept the title of Messiah.

"The Son of Man"

It is noteworthy that, after Peter's confession, when Jesus began to teach them, he does not say that it was necessary for "Christ" to suffer, but very decidedly he remarks that it was necessary for "the Son of Man" to suffer. This constitutes at once a point of agreement as well as of radical departure. He implicitly agrees to being called "the Christ," but he impregnates this word with his own peculiar connotation and does not agree with the popular meaning.

The conception of "the Son of Man" has constituted a very difficult problem in New Testament study. One wonders, while reflecting on it again in the light of modern New Testament research, whether the problem has been finally resolved. Scholars of equal integrity and soundness stand opposed on some important aspects of this central New Testament conception. The English phrase "the Son of Man" as well as the Greek *ho huios tou anthrōpou* do not convey any special meaning. But the corresponding Hebrew and Aramaic words do. It is now regarded with a great deal of probability that the Greek phrase is a word-for-word translation of the Aramaic *Bar-nasha* or *Bar anasha*. The idiomatic translation, of course, would be *ho anthrōpos*. But if this had been used, it would have given rise to much misunderstanding, for it would have been a translation of an uncommon phrase in the original by a very common Greek word. On the other hand, the phrase *ho huios tou anthrōpou* is not at all suitable as a translation, for the word *anthrōpos* in Greek is not a generic term like the Hebrew *ādām* or the Aramaic *anash*.

The Use of the Phrase "The Son of Man"

Dalman says that the Jewish-Palestinian Aramaic of the earlier period has a word *anash*, meaning "a human being." Its singular number *baranash* was not in use, more especially its definite form was quite unheard of in the older Jewish-Aramaic literature. The use of *baranash* or *baranasha* was in-

troduced into Jewish-Galilean and Christian-Palestinian literature from the northeast of Palestine along with many other
influences affecting the use of terms and vocabulary.[16]

Son of Man and Messiah

A question arises whether the Jewish rabbis were in a position to find the relationship between "Messiah" and "the Son
of Man." Dalman seems to suggest that there was a possibility
of their so connecting those concepts, if their Messiah conception was based on Dan., ch. 7. But apparently they seemed
to have failed to do so; therefore "the Son of Man" did not
become a Messianic title.[17] Rudolf Otto says: "He had already
reached the synthesis between the Son of Man and the Servant
of God. In his new *didachē* he now reached the synthesis between the Son of Man and the Suffering Servant of God."[18]
Others, writing about the same words, suggest that a relation
of such terms would not be possible for the Jews. "It certainly
would have never struck a Jew as reasonable to say that these
words could only apply to one person."[19]

This brings us to the point that, if the Jews had not thought
of using this term in relation to the Messiah, and the disciples
of Jesus had not called him by this title but, on the other hand,
invariably give the impression that they had not coined it or
put it into the mouth of Jesus, then the only alternative left is
that he himself applies this title of "the Son of Man" to himself. The fact that the Greek Christians who produced our
Gospels did not apprehend the meaning of the term also is
shown in the fact that they did not introduce it into the pages
of the Gospels.

Many scholars maintain that it is Jesus who uses this term
for himself, first and last. This is true of immediate Gospel
records, of the primitive church and of the church down
through the centuries. This title remains Jesus' own self-desig-
nation — and has been successfully avoided as a name of Jesus
in the theology and the teaching of the church, in the sermons
from the pulpits, and in the lessons in the Sunday schools. It

is also maintained that this is one of the most original things in the life and teaching of Jesus. Thus Dalman, remarking on the self-appellation of Jesus, says: "In all three synoptists *ho huios tou anthrōpou* as the title of Jesus appears only in the words of Jesus himself." [20] Others also confirm this fact. "In the Gospels 'Son of Man' is always found in the mouth of Jesus: it is never used in narrative concerning him. . . . The opinion of the writers of the Gospels is thus clear that Jesus used the phrase, that he used it of himself, and that for unexplained reasons it was not used by his disciples in speaking of him." [21]

The Meaning of "Son of Man"

What is, then, the meaning of the phrase "Son of Man"? Is it an individual or a personal or a corporate term? Concerning "the Son of Man" in the book of Enoch, two views are possible. "As the texts stand now two views are taken of the elect one. According to one (Enoch 48:6), he was 'chosen and hidden before him [God] before the creation of the world and for evermore.' According to the other (Enoch 71:16), Enoch himself is 'that Son of Man.'" [22] These two views are irreconcilable. Dr. R. H. Charles, rejecting the second view as a textual accident, affirms the personal and individual nature of the elect one. Referring to the relation between Jesus and the Enoch tradition, Rudolf Otto says that Jesus lived in the ideas of Enoch's apocalyptic tradition but was not an apocalyptist himself. "Son of Man" was an apocalyptic term that Jesus used to express his mission. "This idea was the form which consciousness of mission necessarily assumed under the condition of his age. We repeat: His consciousness of mission did not issue from such a previously formed idea, but from the constitution and essence of his person." [23] Recently Dr. V. Taylor has shown his agreement with the conclusion of Dr. R. H. Charles. He quotes Dr. Charles (*Book of Enoch*, p. 307) to the effect that: "In Daniel the phrase ["Son of Man"] seems merely symbolical of Israel, but in Enoch it denotes a supernatural person." [24] Dr. Taylor therefore approvingly says that in Enoch as in the Gospels the Son of Man is an individual rather than the "faithful remnant." [25] Over against this, Prof. T. W. Manson develops the thesis that "the Son of Man" in the Gospels is a corporate term, such as "the remnant" in Isaiah, "the servant of Jehovah" in II Isaiah, the "I" of the Psalms, and "the Son of Man" in Daniel. He also holds to the possibility that "the elect one" and "the righteous one" and "the appointed one" are corporate terms even in Enoch. To Manson the "one like the Son of Man" of Dan. 7:13 is equal to "the saints of the Most High" of Dan. 7:22.[26] Kirsopp Lake and F. Foakes-Jackson, while commenting on this phrase in Daniel, seem to agree with Manson when they say that: "The 'man' is not the King of Israel; here, Israel itself, and the only question is whether Israel on earth is not supposed to have a heavenly representative in human form whose exaltation in heaven corresponds to the exaltation of Israel on earth." [27]

The question naturally arises concerning Dr. Manson's thesis, that, if the Son of Man is a corporate term, how is it that Jesus so often uses it for himself? He both raises this question and answers it, saying: "The answer to this question is that the restriction of the denotation of the term is the outcome of the prophetic ministry of Jesus. His mission is to create the Son of Man, the kingdom of the saints of the Most High, to realize in Israel the ideal contained in the term. This task is attempted in two ways: first by public appeal to the people through the medium of parable and sermon and by the mission of the disciples; then, when this appeal produced no adequate response, by the consolidation of his own band of followers. Finally, when it becomes apparent that not even the disciples are ready to rise to the demands of the ideal, he stands alone, embodying in his own person the perfect human response to the regal claims of God." [28] In any case, whatever the disagreements of these scholars may be, they make the ideals taken from Deutero-Isaiah integral to their theses rather than those taken from Ezekiel. By examining the passages in the Synoptics where the term "Son of Man" is used several inferences follow:

1. That the majority of these passages are found after the confession of Peter.
2. That the majority of these passages are addressed to the disciples.
3. That in most of the passages the term " Son of Man " is used in a special sense rather than as " man " in general.
4. That these passages can be divided very conveniently into those dealing with the Passion and those dealing with the Parousia. Mark and L incorporate Passion passages and Q and M those belonging to the Parousia.

The last point of this brief summary shows that the conception of " the Son of Man " includes the ideas both of humiliation and exaltation. The Synoptics in agreement with the rest of the New Testament show that this humiliation and exaltation is primarily of Jesus: but they go beyond this and include in it the humiliation and exaltation of the followers of Jesus. Just as Jesus suffered and died, so also those that are of Jesus in following him passed through the narrow way, took up the cross, and bore in their mortal bodies the marks of the suffering of Christ, thereby filling in the gaps in his suffering. Just as they identified themselves with the suffering and death of Jesus, so also shall they be exalted when he is exalted. " The saints of the Most High " are exalted with Jesus. Thus we find that the conception of the Son of Man is individual and corporate at the same time. It is in Jesus, the Son of Man, that all is subsumed and brought in obedience to God. Thus the Son of Man in the Gospels is the final term fulfilling all the prophetic insights and longings of the past. The Kingdom of God is the Kingdom of Jesus, who is coheir with " the saints of the Most High."

Cullmann, in *The Christology of the New Testament*, surveys the whole question of the Son of Man and concludes that Jesus himself connected *ebed Yahweh* and *Bar-nasha*. In an over-all statement he says, " We conclude from this survey that within the ' Hellenists ' and the group represented by the Gospel of John especially expressed their faith in Jesus (in close connection with his own self-consciousness) by means of the Son of Man concept, and that Paul gave the concept greater theological depth " (p. 188).

It seems that the hitherto divergent views regarding the Son of Man may be converging toward a solution. Bultmann remarks, in his *Theology of the New Testament* (Vol. I, p. 43), that " Jesus' call to decision implies a Christology." This immediately raises the question that if Jesus had this estimate of himself then it is clearly incompatible with the imminent expectation of a different " Son of Man." James Robinson, in his *New Quest of the Historical Jesus* (p. 103), makes a pointed reference to this development in Bultmannian circles. Vincent Taylor, in his commentary on Mark, also expresses a similar hope for the solution of this problem.

" The Son of God "

Unlike the conception of " the Son of Man," Jesus never uses the title " Son of God " for himself; but in spite of this he very convincingly conveys the impression that he does not stand in an ordinary relation of sonship to God but in a very special one. He is not " a son " but " the Son."

Just as the Greek composers of our Gospels read a different meaning into the idea of " the Son of Man " from that intended in the original Hebrew or Aramaic, so also the phrase " Son of God " is open to both Greek and Hebraic interpretation. This divergence of interpretation is made possible through cherishing different views of God as the " Father." Prof. T. W. Manson says: "When the word ' Father ' is used as a name for God, it means primarily either that God is the *fons et origo* of human life, the Father of our spirits, or that he watches over and cares for men and women in a manner analogous to the parental care of a good earthly father. The former is typical of Greek thought, the latter is characteristic of Hebrew, Jewish, and Christian utterances." [29]

The Greek conception is clearly brought out by Luke in the announcement of the angel to Mary and in the geneaology of Jesus, which is traced back to God. The Israelitish distinction is brought out in Deut. 32:6; Isa. 63:16; Mal. 2:10; etc.

The Baptism and the Transfiguration

Of all the utterances in the Synoptics the most important for our consideration are the ones concerning the baptism [30] and the transfiguration.[31] At the baptism the Voice says: "Thou art my beloved Son, in thee I am well pleased." At the transfiguration it says: "This is my beloved Son: hear him." The question arises whether these sayings have any reference to the Old Testament Scriptures, more particularly to Ps. 2. It is probable that Mark did not see any connection with the Old Testament and merely recorded the Voice from heaven as a matter of fact. There has been, no doubt, an attempt to interpret the baptism in the light of Isa. 42:1. "But, possible though this may seem, it is incapable of demonstration, and it is more likely that Mark connected the Voice from heaven with no special passage in the Old Testament." [32]

The first thing that is clear from these passages is that the baptism Voice is meant for Jesus. And the other is meant for the disciples, because they are commanded to "hear him." What happened at the baptism is more of the nature of a coronation ceremony; it is a confirmation of the fact of Sonship which was also later affirmed at the transfiguration. At the baptism "Jesus receives an assurance, the essence of which is contained in the declaration: 'Thou are my Son.' What is given here is not a task to be performed or a message to be delivered, but a status and a relation. At the very outset it is indicated that the central thing in his ministry will be what he is, rather than what he says. As the ministry continues, the message becomes plainer and the task more obvious; but both message and task are still conditioned by the primary fact of Sonship." [33]

What did Jesus understand by "Son of God"? It is clear that Jesus recognizes the difference between himself as the Son

and the others as the servants. This is shown by a comparison
and contrast with John the Baptist.[34] And more clearly in the
parable of the vineyard, where Jesus distinguishes himself as
the Son from the prophets. (Mark 12:1-11.) The Father-
hood of God was a familiar doctrine of Judaism, but it gained
a central position in the Christian economy by the way Jesus
lived it out. To him the Father was the deepest reality of his
being. He seldom spoke about it, and when he did it was only
to the disciples who had a discerning faith. The Father revealed himself to him and the Son responded with perfect love,
obedience, and trust. The complete knowledge of the Father
is the unreserved communion with him, so much so that the
fact is that " no one knoweth who the Son is save the Father,
and who the Father is save the Son and he to whomsoever the
Son wills to reveal him." The full meaning of this fact can be
found only in the mystery of the personality of Jesus and in
the depth of his consciousness. Only those can dimly apprehend it who, being brought into intimate contact with him, are
enabled to address God as *Abba* and thereby become coheirs
of the Kingdom. " The ultimate truth about Jesus is that He is
the Son of God." [35]

" THE CHRIST "

In Jewish thought the Christ, the anointed one, is he who
would rule over the independent Kingdom of Israel under the
protection of God. The idea of redeemer is not linked with
him. It is God who saves and liberates. Only under the influence of some apocryphal sources the idea of the redeemer
is connected with the Messiah. This synthesis apparently was
achieved in and about the time of Jesus.[36]

This title did not become the prerogative title of anyone
until the time of Jesus. Before that anyone anointed and con-
secrated would have the adjective " Messiah." In Jewish thought
the term was used for the scion of the house of David, for the
celestial Son of Man, and for the high priest. But nowhere is
there any indication that the Jews identified one with the other.

So when the disciples of Jesus use this term for him, their meaning should be decided from the context.

It is probable that in no passage relevant to the term is Jesus called *Christos* in Q. The use of the word in Mark is also rare, yet Mark does not leave anybody in doubt that *Christos* was a title of Jesus.[37] In Matt. 27:17, 22, a phrase "Jesus surnamed Christ" is used, like "Simon who is surnamed Peter." This certainly belongs to the later strata, where *Christos* became another name for Jesus, although the title also remained.[38] But in the lifetime of Jesus "Messiah" probably never became his surname. Dalman says, "It cannot, however, be supposed that during his earthly life Jesus ever bore the title 'Messiah' as a surname." [39] Dalman also points out that *Christos Kyrios* as a title of the Messiah cannot possibly be a mistranslation from the original.

In the confession of Peter, as we have observed previously, there is a certain disparity between what Peter thinks the Messiah should be like and what Jesus thinks him to be. Jesus tells Peter that "the Son of Man" must suffer, and this obviously throws Peter off his feet, for he evidently expects the triumphant nationalistic Messiah. But even this context fails to make fully clear whether "the Son of Man" is the scion of David. The Christians, however, seem to have found in Jesus both "the Son of Man" and "the scion of the house of David." This does not seem to be suggested either by the two figures being identified or by the fact that the title "anointed one" was applied to one person. It also seems likely that the idea of the Son of David was added to that of "the Son of Man" rather than vice versa. The fact of a resurrection might have brought about his synthesis in the minds of the Christians, although David calling his son his Lord seems to cast doubt on the whole idea of Davidic expectation.

Jesus also himself acknowledged that he was the Messiah. In the confession of Peter, although he corrects Peter and aligns himself with the prophetic category over against the apocalyptic, he never for a moment disowns being called

"Messiah." So Jesus, by first acknowledging himself to be the Son of Man; secondly, by giving assent to Peter's calling him "Messiah"; and finally not denying himself to be such before the high priest and before Pilate, at the time of his trial, unambiguously affirms that he is the Messiah — *ho Christos*.

Kyrios, Didaskalos, Rabbi

Matthew and Luke show a decided predilection for *Kyrios* over Mark and Q. As a matter of fact, the word is not used at all in Mark with the exception of ch. 7:28. By the evidence of I Cor. 16:22 it is demonstrated that the word *Maran*, which means "our Lord," was used by the Aramaic-speaking Christians. It was an appellative of respect, like the Greek *Kyrie*. The Syriac of the Old Testament has a different word for God. It is *Marya*, over against *Maran*. This word *Maran* therefore could easily be translated into Greek as *Kyrios* or *Kyrios hēmōn*.

The Gospels and The Acts clearly show that *Kyrios* belongs only to the later strata of the tradition, and the earlier and usual title for Jesus is *Rabbi*, which is translated into the Greek as *Didaskalos*. Both Matthew and Luke show a peculiar dislike for *Didaskalos* and *Rabbi*. In Luke several times the words *Didaskalos* and *Rabbi* are replaced by *Epistata*, i.e., "Master." It is, however, true that *Didaskalos* and not *Kyrios* is the more primitive title of Jesus.

The possible conclusion may be that among his immediate and personal followers in and about Jerusalem he was known as *Rabbi*, "Teacher," and not as *Maran*. This attitude is reflected by Mark and Q. But there were Aramaic-speaking Christians outside Jerusalem, probably at Antioch, where *Maran*, or *Mari*, was current, and they addressed Jesus as *Maran* or *Mari*. This attitude is reflected by M and L. Later on, this was translated into Greek by *Kyrios* in which language it was playing a dominant part at that time. The influence of the Septuagint should not be disregarded, because it certainly lent support to the meaning of the word. Thus "the divine attributes of the Lord Jehovah passed over to the Lord Jesus." [40]

So, when the Christians addressed Jesus as "Lord," they implied that he is the true Lord over against the false imperial gods and lords of Rome. Luke even uses the phrase *Christos Kyrios* (Luke 2:11), and makes his language inclusive enough to apply it to the Messiah. On the other hand, the Jews could not develop any such terminology with regard to the Messiah, because they could not dare attribute to Messiah a place equal to God. [41]

THE FOURTH GOSPEL

This Gospel has been alternatively interpreted from the Greek or Jewish background. Both elements are present in the Gospel and its relation to its background is not simple. C. K. Barrett remarks in the beginning of his commentary on the Gospel that, "the coexistence of these two strains of thought recalls their earlier combination in Hellenistic Judaism; but whatever precedents may be invoked, it cannot be maintained that the background of the Gospel (and a fortiori its relation to its background) is simple."

A word should be said about the relation of this Gospel to the Synoptics. It is now generally recognized that the writer of this Gospel knew about both the Gospels of Mark and Luke, perhaps Mark more than Luke. There is no evidence to show that he was conversant with Matthew's Gospel. This shows that there is no absolute gulf between this Gospel and the others, and that some common tradition is present to show the degree of dependence and relationship.

The unity of this Gospel has been doubted, but the trend of scholarship at the present time is very decisive in affirming its unity and integrity. However, it is still open to question whether it is a seamless robe or not!

The Logos

For our purpose, however, the Logos conception is of great importance. Since it occurs in the Prologue, a word or two concerning it would not be out of place here. Some scholars have maintained, and Harnack is chief among them, that the Prologue is an afterthought and does not stand in relationship of unity with the rest of the Gospel. With this, of course, modern scholars, Streeter, Dodd, and others, do not agree. They regard the Prologue as essential to the Gospel and maintain that although the word *Logos* does not occur in any other place outside the Prologue, nevertheless the thought and the theme of the Prologue is present throughout the whole Gospel.

Rendel Harris maintains "that St. John in his Prologue was working from existing materials, which comprise the Praises of Sophia in the Sapiential Books, and perhaps from some Sophia songs that are no longer extant." [42] To him the Prologue is a hymn to Sophia, with the word *Logos* substituted for it. C. F. Burney has tried to show that it is a hymn to the Logos originally composed in Aramaic. Its Hebraic style and arrangement of words is an illustration of "climactic parallelism." [43] This marks it not as Greek but as Hebrew poetry.

Much has been written about the Logos and much effort has been exerted in finding out the origin of the concept. Most of this has been futile and has not led to valid results. C. F. Burney maintains that the Logos conception is not of Alexandrian origin but belongs to Palestinian-Jewish thought. In his opinion "the Logos conception of the Prologue must undoubtedly be derived from the third and most frequent Targumic conception representing God in manifestation; that of the *Memra deva*, 'the Word of the Lord.'" [44] He goes on to suggest that we should trace *Memra* to the Old Testament passages where the Hebrew word *dabar* is used. G. F. Moore, however, regards this view erroneous and says that it is "not employed in the Targums in the rendering of such Hebrew phrases as 'the word (*dabar*) of the Lord,' the 'Word of God,' 'My Word,' 'Thy Word,' etc." [45] To him it is a "buffer word," "a phenomenon of translation," or, as Canon Streeter has said, a "verbal smoke screen." This being its usage and function, he goes on to say: "But nowhere in the Targums is

Memra a ' being ' of any kind or in any sense, much less a personal being. The appearance of personality, which in some passages attaches to the word, is due solely to the fact that the *memra* of the Lord and similar phrases are reverent circumlocutions for ' God,' introduced precisely where in the original God is personally active in the affairs of men; and personal character of the activity necessary adheres to the periphrasis." [46]

This, of course, does not mean that there is no basis whatsoever for the Logos conception in Jewish thought. As a matter of fact, the Jews held a doctrine of the Word which passed through several stages. The Word of God is charged with power to accomplish the desired task (Isa. 51:16). So also the Word of God in the mouth of the prophet of God is charged with power. (Jer. 1:9 ff.) The concept of the Word in Jewish thought is dominated by the idea that God is so "holy" that he cannot be involved in the affairs of the world. But when the affairs of Israel became more complex the notion of the creative Word was absorbed into the idea of Wisdom (Ps. 33:6; 147:15). Wisdom is coexistent with God. (Prov. 8:22 ff.) Wisdom is presented here in poetic personification. Later, under the influence of Greek thought, Wisdom assumed the role of an intermediary. The transcendent God created things through the agency of Wisdom and other intermediaries. " The transcendence, however, is moral and not metaphysical. The presence of the intermediary beings is intended to emphasize that God is always a living God, who does things in the world and for his people." [47] This Wisdom of God was ultimately identified with the Torah. The Torah is from heaven and the agent through which God created the world. [48]

So it becomes abundantly clear that the Johannine Logos in the sense of the spoken Word of God is rooted and grounded in Jewish thought. But does John use the word *Logos* only in this sense, or is it more inclusive? If John used this word only in this restricted sense, then he would have to have recourse to the idea of intermediaries in one form or another. But he is very emphatic in saying that "all things were made by him; and without him was not anything made that hath been made." This statement does away at one stroke with every conception of an intermediary being. But one question remains. Does the word *Logos*, which ordinarily has two meanings, mean something more in addition to what has been explained just now? Does it also imply an immanent, rational principle of unity and cohesion? It is true that this thought is more or less explicit in Colossians and Hebrews, but John does not make any clear statement, although the thought is present in John 1:10.[49] It can be safely assumed that the Jewish-Hellenistic readers of John were familiar with both conceptions, and that although John does not lose sight of one or the other conception, his inclination is clearly toward the Hebrew conception.

Philo, the Jewish-Alexandrian philosopher who died in A.D. 54, effected a synthesis between the Hebrew idea of the Logos and the Stoic conception of the immanent reason derived from Heraclitus' Logos, the divine law. According to Philo, God is a solitary being who does not have any partners. Like other powers and attributes of God the Logos is a mode of the divine essence and not that essence itself. God transcends the Logos just as he transcends and exhausts other attributes. The Logos is the oldest of the intelligible beings, and in that respect is called the "second God," the archetype, the Son, the image and the seal, and the divine rational energy. This idea of ideas, the Logos, creates the universe as an architect by impressing its image upon formless matter. Man is also an image of this archetype. He does not say that the Logos is the "uttered word" of God, for God has no organs like man to speak with. This Logos as the divine energy gives form and cohesion to the chaotic matter and links the cosmos to the infinite source of power and order. But the Logos is not different from the macrocosm as well as from the microcosm; it is coextensive with them. It is different only because it is immaterial and can be apprehended only through the intellect. Those who are imperfect and cannot truly apprehend the first God are asked to worship the second God — the Logos. But this does not mean that Philo is suggesting a subordinate divine being. As a good monotheist he would disclaim any statement like that. "No doubt he would have done so had he supposed that the world was a mere fabric put together by God. But he viewed it as a tissue of divine forces; and therefore those who worshiped it as God held not so much a false as an imperfect view. The Logos, the cosmic principle in the material universe, was really divine, being the rational energy, the formative thought of God, and consequently it was not by a mere figure of speech that it was spoken of as God." [50] Yet it was necessary to distinguish it from God, because it was immanent and the expression rather than transcendent and the cause.

According to Wolfson,[51] there are three stages in the existence of the Logos: (1) as property of God; (2) as the totality of the created incorporeal powers; and (3) as the totality of the powers of God existing within the world itself (*Philo,* Vol. I, pp. 327, etc.).

The Logos is looked upon as the high priest in the visible and perceptible cosmos. This cosmos is the temple of God. Philo's Logos in this capacity of the high priest is the suppliant Logos. Some have suggested that Philo here presents a personal Logos. But on a closer thought it becomes hard to hold such a view. The Logos, being coextensive with the perceptible cosmos, cannot supplicate for anybody, for doing so would beg the question. But the "supplication" may be some sort of plea for further light. "Reason coming from God to man has the character of an ambassador, proclaiming the divine requirements; in ascending from man to God it assumes the guise of a suppliant, praying for fuller light and purer wisdom from the infinite Giver." [52]

Philo's Logos is not personal, but rather rational energy flowing from the being of God and pervading the cosmos, acting as a means (in the sense of principle) through which the essence of personality is communicated from the Infinite to his finite children. At the best it is a poetic personification.

It may safely be concluded that Philo was unable to conceive of a personal Logos. His Hebrew background could not allow him to posit another personal existence alongside his lonely God who reigns in solitary majesty; whereas, his alliance with Greek thought would not permit him to make friends with the "scandal of particularity." The idealist view would not allow its immanent and pervasive divine Logos to wed the unique and the particular. It can, however, use the particular as a vehicle of expression, but in that case the particular is not necessary to it. It can be left behind, discarded or transcended.

The Gospel of John opens with the phrase "in the beginning was the Word." This reminds one of the opening words of the book of Genesis. But the Evangelist takes us farther back. The Logos who certainly is present at the beginning is, as Temple says, "at the root of the universe." The Logos of John, like the wisdom of Proverbs but unlike the Logos of Philo, is pre-existent and coeternal with God. "And the Word was with God." This clause implies distinct persons in communication. The word *Pros* should be translated in the sense of "over against-ness," and not to imply that the Logos is absorbed in God. The relationship is mutual, but mutuality of relationship presupposes distinct personal existence. The Logos therefore is related to God yet distinct from him. "And the Word was God." The word "God" does not have the definite article, therefore "God" should be taken as an adjective. This indicates the divinity of the Logos. The Logos of John is eternal, personal, and divine.

In verse 3, the positive and negative phrases are an example of Hebrew parallelism. The Evangelist says, "All things were made by him." In this the Evangelist tries to show that the Logos is the sole agent with total power of creation. There is no eternal matter as Philo presupposes, and also there are no intermediary agents of creation. "God's instrument of creation was the word of power in which he uttered himself." [53]

Verse 10, by asserting that "he was in the world," links up with the first verse and demonstrates the continuous existence

of the Logos who was immanent in the world before the incarnation.

"And the world was made by him, and the world knew him
not." The world did not recognize the immanent Logos. This
language reminds one of similar language of Heraclitus, who
thinks that the people do not show any understanding of the
eternal Logos. And though all things run according to the
Logos yet people are ignorant of it. In spite of this similarity
of language, John's thought goes far beyond the impersonal
Logos of the Greek thinker.

In the fourteenth verse John makes the most staggering
statement — "and the Word became flesh, and dwelt among
us." It is staggering because it is not warranted by either his
Jewish or Greek background. This is John's most unique contribution to Christian thought. He identifies the eternal, divine
Word with a human person — the concrete reality of human
nature in its totality. He identifies the Word with Jesus Christ.
The word "became" does not refer to the process but rather
to the statement. "And the Word became flesh" is a judgment
based on the experience of the Evangelist. He is bearing witness
to an empirical fact (I John 1:1-3). "And dwelt among us"
dispels the doubt of the incarnation being some form of
Docetism. The dwelling of "the Word became flesh" in our
midst is real and existential. The idea of the Tabernacle is also
present in this context, bearing out a certain unity between the
Old and the New Testament.

John in his bold utterance has transcended all the previous
formulations of the Logos. He has shown their inadequacy. In
"the Word became flesh" John has resolved the polarities of
existence — God and the world; eternity and time; infinity and
finitude; grace and sin; light and darkness; life and death; love
and hate.

C. H. Dodd in his famous commentary on the Fourth Gospel
comes to the conclusion that the statements, "And the Word
was God" and "The Word became flesh" are original with

John and could not be anticipated from the Jewish and Hellenistic background of the Gospel.

The Father and the Son

The Father-Son relationship is one of the major notes of this Gospel. The question, however, arises whether this relationship is metaphysical or moral and spiritual. The first verse of the Prologue certainly gives us a metaphysical basis. To say " and the Word was God " is to assert essential relationship. He is very God of very God. In spite of the presence of such a thought, the rest of the Gospel seems to approach the question of the Father-Son relationship from the moral and the spiritual standpoint. It is true that fourth-century controversialists dealt with the question from the point of view of *ousia*. Some believe that John 1:13 ("which were born, not of blood, nor of the will of the flesh, nor of the will of man, but of God") is the Johannine version of the virgin birth. Temple says that it does not matter whether the verb is "who was born" or its plural: the implication of virgin birth is clear.[54] C. F. Burney, who assumes the Aramaic origin of the Gospel, says that the different readings arise because of the insertion or omission of an Aramaic particle. He prefers the singular reading, and translates "inasmuch as He was born, not of blood, nor of the will of the flesh, nor of the will of man, but of God": i.e., he, being born not after the manner of flesh, but of God, was thus able to give to those who received him power to become sons of God.[55] He also believes that the passage in question refers to the virgin birth. Macgregor, commenting on Burney's thesis, says, "But even if this reading be accepted, it is hardly true to say with Burney that the writer is drawing out the mystical import of the virgin birth, for the words in question would exclude the idea of human mother no less than of human father." [56]

Let us then look at the question from the moral and the spiritual angle. This may be done in three ways: (1) That the

Son is representative, and that the Father is present in the Son;[57] (2) As a common activity of the Father and the Son in which the Father shares the Son's functions, as is brought out in John 17:10: "And all things that are mine are thine, and thine are mine: and I am glorified in them"; [58] (3) The Son's utter dependence on the Father, as is shown in John 12:49: "For I spake not from myself; but the Father which sent me, he hath given me a commandment, what I should say, and what I should speak." [59]

Let us take a saying that is typical of Father-Son relationship and discuss it briefly. In John 10:30, Jesus says, "I and my Father are one." This is a very terse and powerful saying, and in a concise way mirrors the mind of Jesus. If we follow the line of patristic interpretation, we would be led to believe that the verse signifies the unity of essence of two distinct persons. But modern critics hold that this interpretation does not do justice to the thought of the writers of the first century. For the fathers, quite contrary to the intention both of the Evangelist and of Jesus, read their metaphysical presuppositions into this dramatic saying and made a case for the identity between Father and Son. The relationship, on the other hand, is of filial intimacy and dependence. Through consummate obedience to the will of the Father, the Son has the oneness of intimacy and love with him, so much so that his will is not his will but his Father's. This is not to say that the Son does not have his own will, but rather that in practical day-to-day living the Son's will is so perfectly attuned to the Father's that for practical observation there is no difference between his will and his Father's, although ontologically there are two wills. This, of course, would not be possible without conscious dependence upon the Father. This oneness, therefore, is the oneness of love and dependence. And love and dependence are not opposed concepts. The Father's will is the deepest reality of the life of Jesus, and the knowledge of this reality is gained by direct love relationship and conscious dependence. The unity is the unity of mind, of will, and of purpose. This is the meaning of Sonship, and this is the content of his filial consciousness. Thus he is unique and *sui generis* and human beings can become the sons of God through him and him alone.

" No man hath seen God at any time; the only begotten Son, which is in the bosom of the Father, he hath declared him." (John 1:18.) Hence the purpose of John's Gospel is " that ye may believe that Jesus is the Christ, the Son of God; and that believing ye may have life in his name " (John 20:31).

Both Dodd and Cullmann connect the Logos with the Son of Man. There are frequent references to the Son of Man in the Gospel. Perhaps Cullmann in his *The Christology of the New Testament* overdraws the picture of the Son of Man in relation to Logos. The crucial point is that the Logos is not confined to the Prologue, but through its internal connection with the Son of Man pervades the Gospel. By the same token the Son of Man concept is present in the Prologue.

RECONSTRUCTION OF NEW TESTAMENT CHRISTOLOGY: THE DIVINITY

The word " reconstruction " as applied to the materials of the New Testament may mean a modern man's attempt at systematization and therefore a cruel and rough handling of the data of the New Testament, which were never meant to be so treated. The picture of the Christ of the New Testament writers is first and foremost due to their faith. The word " faith " here does not mean a caprice that gives rise to a fiction divorced from facts — that the apostles had a poetic license for indulging in imaginary arrangements of ideas. Their faith is the experience of the factual in relation to the eternal. Their experience is constituted of fact and interpretation, inseparable and integral. At the center of their faith stand the cross and the resurrection. They experienced salvation by being crucified, buried, and raised with their Lord and Savior.[60] They who once were estranged from the life of God are reconciled to him through the life and death of Jesus Christ. The New Testament critics in their attempts to get behind the Gospel tradition are

trying to separate fact from interpretation, the historical from
the eternal. They may be able to succeed to some degree, but
a completely historical portrait of Jesus Christ may be beyond
the power and the scope of the New Testament criticism, inasmuch as he is not anywhere presented in that fashion. It is
hard to draw the line between the Jesus of history and the
Christ of faith.

Furthermore, the writers of the New Testament were not
directly conscious of intellectual inconsistencies. They never set
before themselves the task of intellectual interpretation. Their
presentation is not step by step and does not submit to the
rigid demands of logic. Theirs is the testimony and witness to
what they saw, handled, and experienced, even the Word of
God. The reason why the apostolic writers did not have the
same problem as we have now is that Jesus Christ was not re-
mote from the actual experience, and the total impact of the
Master's personality was profound and integral. In the face of
the empirical unity of the life of Christ and their experience of
it, immediate or mediate, there was no room whatsoever for
raising irreconcilable issues. So even now, wherever the apostolic experience is recaptured, the difficulty of a rational synthesis is not felt. Nevertheless, it is true that when we analyze the
New Testament experience of the Person of Jesus Christ we
come face to face with problems that seem to be more than a
match for our intellects. With this side of the problem we shall
deal in a different section. We shall here summarize the view
of the New Testament writers regarding the divinity of Jesus
Christ.

It may be said safely on the basis of our study that no sharp
differences exist among the New Testament writers. There are
no Christologies in the New Testament. There is only one
Christology subject to two modifications. The first modification
is that there is a certain logical evolution of thought. This may
be noticed if we examine the logical sequence of thought from
the Synoptists through Paul and The Letter to the Hebrews to
John. None of them introduces an absolutely new idea which

is not present in one form in the others, and yet there is steady growth and development of ideas. There is also a steady grouping together of loose threads of thought. The second modification is that the writers write with a different emphasis and in their own peculiar way. This is so because they write under the limitations of their own personal peculiarities and the type and the need of the situation to which they address themselves. Now if we were to consider each one apart from the others, we might find some justification for building up a case for different Christologies in the New Testament. But if on the other hand, we look at the whole of the New Testament from the point of view of that which is common to it all, not by a process of abstraction, but by actually finding it out, we will be assured that it is one and the same person that they are talking about. The old distinction between Paulinism and the religion of Jesus, and the Johannine theology and the synoptic history, is no longer valid. We thank the New Testament critics for this very valuable service.

The New Testament view of the divinity of Christ can be understood in a twofold manner: (1) metaphysical and (2) historical.

The presupposition of the metaphysical view is that Christ is of the same nature as God. The writers either directly or by implication state this truth clearly. He is coeternal with God and he subsists in a relationship of communion with him. He is the image of the invisible God, first-born before all creation. He is the effulgence of God's glory and the express image of his character. He is the Son of God and so, very God of very God. This Eternal, whose days begin with the days of God, is also the creator of the universe. There is nothing in the existing universe which is not his handiwork. He does not undertake this creative activity because he is simply a passive instrument in the hand of God. He himself is the hand of God. He himself creates with life and power and light. The created universe is not left to itself after creation; it still coheres in him. By the word of his power he upholds it. There are no rival powers and intermediary agents of creation and subsistence. He is also immanent and is the source of man's light and knowledge of truth. He is the basis of the fact that God has not left any nation without witness and that the Logos was in the world and the world knew it not — the same eternal Logos, the Son of God, and the image of the invisible God became flesh. He became flesh for two reasons: to reveal the mind and will of God the Father to man, and to reconcile God and man, nay, God and the world. In the incarnation God reconciles himself to the world and the world to himself.

The presupposition of the historical view is that one who does the will of God is the Son of God. The Hebrew conception of Sonship is different from the Greek, which is physical and then metaphysical. The Hebrew conception is based on a moral relationship of responsibility, care, and of obedience. The basis and the clue to this view is the filial consciousness of Jesus Christ. There is a growth in the filial relationship. It is said of him that, just as he grew in stature, so also he grew in the knowledge of God and in the favor of God and man. At baptism the Voice calls him the Son of God. This is more of the nature of affirmation and a coronation ceremony than the assignment of a task. His whole life is from first to last the life of obedience, of trust, and of loyalty to the will of God. There is uninterrupted traffic between his soul and God the Father. This is made manifest in his perfect obedience — obedience which through the Garden of Gethsemane leads him to the cross. He and his Father are one, and this unity is unity of will and purpose. It is to fulfill his Father's will and to carry out his purpose that he says, "Not my will but thy will be done," and mounts the cross at Calvary. Christ is the Son of God because he lived his life in perfect obedience, love, and dependence upon his Father's will. After his death on the cross there is the resurrection. The resurrection entitles him to be the Son of God because he is the first-born from the dead. "Thou art my Son, this day have I begotten thee" is quoted in The Acts and The Letter to the Hebrews in the context of the resurrection directly or implicitly.[61] This risen one, the first-born among the dead, the Son of God is also the heavenly man, the quickening Spirit and the Lord and the Christ. He is the Lord because he has conquered every enemy, even death. He thus sums up all things in himself and presents them to God, and he himself is also subjected to him — so that God may be all in all.

It is quite evident that if we allow these views to follow their logical course, the metaphysical would mean some kind of theophany and the historical some kind of deification. But strange to say, the Evangelists never make this mistake. We might read our own preconceived ideas into the New Testament and pronounce the writers guilty, but an objective and impartial look at the New Testament will prove that the apostles and Evangelists never fall into the trap of either heresy. The danger of heresy arises when we relate these views on a rational and schematic basis. The writers of the New Testament refrained from doing so, not that they had a choice, but because they found these views held together without any touch of artificiality in the person and life of their Master, the impact of whose life on theirs had renewed and transformed them. They, therefore, did not look at the life of Christ from a balcony seat but rather from an existential standpoint, because, for better or for worse, for life or for death, their destinies were inseparably dependent upon him. " To whom shall we go? thou hast the words of eternal life." They, therefore, looking at these two intellectually contradictory aspects of the Master's life from the *locus* of *en Christo* found them related together in the living unity of their Savior's life. In his life these two were resolved. But one would not be wrong in one's judgment in saying that if the New Testament writers at any time had preferred to look at the life of Christ from the point of view of a rational synthesis, they would have, in that case, at one time or another fallen into some heresy. In that case the New Testament would have become a piece of human reasoning and not the word of the living God. In what the writers present to us, then, lies the eternal meaning and invitation of the Gospel.

But this raises a difficult problem that we cannot afford to discuss here. The problem is: Does Biblical theology rule out dogmatic theology? Or probably, is dogmatic theology made a branch of Christian apologetics? Or is there a greater possibility of co-ordination between Biblical and dogmatic theology because of the application of principles of various types of criticism to the Biblical text? These questions at present have to remain unanswered. The problem clearly stated is, however, that we have a choice between a paradox and some kind of metaphysics. Concerning whether there is a halfway house between the two, the road signs of synthesis are not clear.

A question needs to be asked at this point. How did the disciples (speaking in the broad sense of the term) come to think of Jesus Christ as the eternal, the image of the invisible, and the Logos, etc.? This is a very hard question to answer. But the answer must lie in the direction in which we have been looking. There is no reason to believe that the godhead of Christ was an assumption of the a priori type with the disciples. Was it then a posteriori? It is true that pure empiricism is no way out. Yet what we have is a fellowship between the disciples and the Master. A fellowship that is true reconciliation, for the experience of salvation shows that the middle wall of partition has been broken down and that God and man are reconciled. In this fellowship somehow or other the disciples get a close look into the Master's personality. To put it in another way, the Master creates in them the sense of appreciation by which alone he can be appreciated. Through their faith, which is the organ of experience by which they had experienced things temporal and eternal in relation with each other, they confronted in their Master authority that could not be deduced or found anywhere else. He forgives sins, which none other than God can do. He is the Lord of the Sabbath. He is the one who says, "Moses says that, but I say this." This is the voice of authority, the very authority of God. Add to these his infinite compassion and love, his miracles and signs. All this, and the day-to-day living with him, and above all, the experience of the resurrection led the disciples to believe in a very realistic way that the one who speaks to them speaks with the authority of God and that the one who overcomes death is the Lord of life.

This is probably the way they traveled; but how exactly they did it is hard to answer. This may be an inference; but it is an existential inference, the knowledge of which is gained through revelation by encountering God in him. Therefore any theoretical sense that attaches to the word " inference " is out of place. And the philosophies of " as if " and the systems of value judgments have to be evaluated from this perspective.

THE HUMANITY OF JESUS CHRIST

THE PAULINE WRITINGS

THE QUESTION of the humanity of our Lord is as important as that of his divinity. We cannot afford to overemphasize the one at the expense of the other. A genuine understanding of Jesus Christ is possible only if the inquirer keeps the total life of the Master before him without allowing either aspect to fade out of the perspective.

Scholars and thinkers have tried many times to reduce the actuality of Jesus to a mere myth. Their laborious efforts, which were rigidly selective in view of the theories they wanted to prove, only obscured the historicity of Christ. The branch of Biblical criticism called "form criticism" has led to the rediscovery of the Jesus of history by expurgating from the Gospels the insertions and redactions. Whether it can be claimed that the Jesus of pure history has become accessible to us is extremely debatable, but that our faith in his historicity has been restored is not questionable.[1]

It is true that Paul is preoccupied in his epistles with the presentation to the outside world of Jesus Christ as the exalted and risen Lord; but to assume on this basis that Paul is not concerned about the humanity of Christ is to treat him lightly and to ignore the empirical development of ideas. Paul shows his concern for the "heavenly man," the "quickening Spirit," only because he has accepted and believed in the humanity of the "Lord of glory." "Therefore for the future we know no one simply as a man. Even if we have known Christ simply as a man, now we do so no longer " (II Cor. 5:16) — this has led some to think that Paul was not interested in the human side of our Lord's life and that he even did not know anything about it. This view should now be regarded as erroneous. But, on the other hand, this verse has received different interpretations. Anderson Scott says, " That Paul had at least seen Jesus, and that he remembered it, is at least one of the possible interpretations of 2 Corinthians v. 16." [2] Maurice Goguel, however, thinks that such an interpretation is not possible. He says: " It must be added that if Paul had known Jesus he would have been among His chief enemies. Why should he who accuses himself of persecuting the disciples not have said that he had fought against the Master himself? " [3] This, of course, does not mean that Paul possessed no knowledge of the historical Christ. It is probable that Paul learned from many sources. His persecutions of the Christian church, which presuppose accusations against the Christians, would certainly imply knowledge of the beliefs and practices of his victims. Associations with the immediate disciples and other Christians from whom he must have secured traditions concerning the life of Christ are more than probable (Gal. 2:6; 1:17-18). In his missionary journeys he may have met people who told him something new about his Master's life. This means that Paul did not get this information from the Gospels. By the time the Gospels were written out and circulated Paul was dead. " And even if we pushed back to problematical sources of the Gospels we cannot assign any collected form to such materials earlier than A.D. 50, by which time Paul was in the full course of his missionary career." [4] Paul, on the other hand, in Gal. 1:12 says, " For indeed it was not from man that I received or learned it, but by a revelation from Jesus Christ." Rawlinson says: " The real point in the argument in Galatians is to establish St. Paul's independence of the Twelve: he had not been their convert, he had never sat at their feet as a catechumen receiving instruction, he had been converted by a direct ' revelation,' he had received his authority immediately from Christ." [5]

Now let us see what Paul does know about the life of Jesus. According to him Jesus was "born of a woman, born subject to law" (Gal. 4:4). It is generally agreed among scholars that Paul here neither discusses nor waives aside the question of the virgin birth. He is not concerned about the virgin birth in either way. Anderson Scott suggests that "subject to the law" refers possibly to circumcision.[6] This is also open to wider interpretation. Lightfoot says "for though Jesus was born under the Mosaic law, the application of the principle is much wider." [7] Jesus had James and other brothers (Gal. 1:19; I Cor. 9:5), "and by descent belonged to the family of David" (Rom. 1:3). To all outward appearances he is a man. (Rom. 5:15-17.) He is obedient and even obedient to the cross. (Rom. 5:19.) G. O. Griffith says that "He was obedient in a still deeper way and more particular sense. He was obedient not only to the law of Moses and to the law of God after which it was patterned, but also to the specific, particular will of God in relation to His own life and ministry." [8] He ate the last meal with his disciples before he was betrayed. (I Cor. 11:23-24.) He was crucified for our sin; he who did not have any sin in him. He was buried and rose from the dead on the third day. (I Cor. 15:3-4.) This gives us an idea of how much Paul did know about the life of our Lord. This broad outline of the life of the historical Jesus is indeed indispensable to the apostle's teaching on salvation and redemption.

By observing the ethical teaching of Paul one would find, in addition to a few quotations, a deeper agreement and correspondence of thought with the teaching of Jesus. The brilliant and outspoken instance of such a case is Rom., ch. 12, where one is impressed by an unmistakable unity with the Master's teaching.[9] Anderson Scott remarks about the teaching of Paul that "the difference of form is so great as to preclude any suggestion of quotation, while the correspondence of thought is too close to allow of independence." [10]

Furthermore, Paul by the guidance of the Spirit of God and

by meditating with prayer over the materials pertaining to the life of Christ derives some significant inferences. His inspired mind with the aptness of a genius discloses the inner life of his Master and thereby affords us a look into the inner character of Jesus which is not available in the Synoptics. He refers to his grace and says: "For you know the grace of our Lord Jesus Christ—how for your sakes He became poor, though He was rich, in order that you through His poverty might become rich." (II Cor. 8:9.) He registers the "obedience" which was characteristic of Jesus; his "disinterestedness" and "purity"; his "deference" and "considerateness," the fact that "he pleased not himself.[11]

It now becomes clear that Paul's emphasis on the risen Lord is not based on his ignorance or dislike of the humanity, but rather his emphasis gains validity from this presupposition. It is his experience of inner liberation and freedom from sin that makes him preach the crucified and the risen Lord with characteristic power and zeal.

The Epistle to the Hebrews

The writer of this epistle gives us a clear and vivid picture of the humanity of our Lord. There is not all that one would like to know, but whatever he does say is enough to bring home to us the actuality and realism of the Master's historical existence. He has a novel way of saying a thing and also of explicating what he means in several ways.

The writer quite a few times addresses the Master by his private name "Jesus" (Heb. 2:9). This simple description has the merit of introducing the reader informally to the High Priest of the New Covenant. One also gets the feeling quite unconsciously that the person thus introduced is a real and living being.

The writer maintains that the person who is called Jesus became man; and the answer to *Cur Deus Homo?* is that he became man in order to save man from sin (Heb. 2:9). He came to help the descendants of Abraham, and not angels or stocks or stones. (Heb. 2:16.) He resembled his brothers, the human beings. (Heb. 2:11.) He also called them his brothers and thereby claimed a deeper kinship with them. This High Priest who ministered to the needs of sinful man did not hail from the stock of Aaron. He sprouted forth from the family tree of the tribe of Judah. (Heb. 7:14.)

The writer pictures Jesus as the preacher and the announcer of the message of salvation. In this historical perspective of the declaration of the kerygma the Lord himself is first. (Heb. 2:3a.) In the second place the truth of what the Lord said was made sure to the hearers by those who were his immediate hearers, i.e., his immediate disciples. (Heb. 2:3b.) And furthermore, the testimony of the disciples before the world was corroborated by the presence and the power of the Holy Spirit. (Heb. 2:4.) This leads us to the idea of the community produced by this process. This the writer presupposes because he is writing to such a community. This is clear and simple history. Such a portrait would defy any association with myth or fiction.

This author does not give us any information about the accusations of the Jews against Jesus and about his religious and civil trials. But the reason is plain — he dies for the sin of man. It is not hard to read between the lines and infer that Christ dies the death of a criminal. He was crucified outside the gates of the city of Jerusalem. (Heb. 13:12.) Capital punishments were always inflicted outside the city in the ancient world. The writer here is not emphasizing the historical, but rather the symbolic, element. This, however, does not invalidate the crude fact of the crucifixion outside the city gates. On the figurative side of the verse Moffatt remarks: "Crucifixion, like the other capital punishments, in the ancient world was inflicted outside the city. To the writer this fact seems intensely significant, rich in symbolism. So much so that his mind hurries on to use it, no longer as a mere confirmation of the negative in v. 10, but a positive fresh call to unworldliness. All such sensuous ideas as those implied in sacrificial meals mix up our religion with the very world from which we ought, after Jesus, to be withdrawing. We meet Jesus outside all this, not inside it." [12]

Next, the author places Jesus in the rough-and-tumble of human life, stormed with temptations and beset with weaknesses. He is man among men and placed in their environment by virtue of sharing their perishable nature. (Heb. 2:14.) The verse " For we have not a High Priest who is unable to feel for us in our weaknesses, but one who was tempted in every respect, just as we are tempted and yet did not sin " probably anticipates an objection that this High Priest being so holy is hereby unable to feel with us in our infirmities. (Heb. 4:15.) This objection is answered by saying that he was tempted like a man in every way and even then remained without sin. From this two conclusions follow: first, that he is able not only to sympathize with us, but to feel with us as if our weaknesses are his, short only of experiencing our sins. Bishop Westcott says: " It expresses not simply the compassion of one who regards suffering from without, but the feeling of one who enters into the suffering and makes it his own." [13] Secondly, in spite of temptations he remained sinless. This is the further reason for his ability to feel for us. For he has not fallen where we have. Moffatt says that it " is a real ground for encouragement, for the best help is that offered by those who have stood where we slip and faced the onset of temptation without yielding to it." [14]

It is true that " weaknesses are the sources of temptations "; so the words " tempted in every respect " seem to exclude some sources of temptations. In our case some of our worst temptations arise because of the sins previously committed. This in the case of Jesus is not true. Bishop Westcott says, " We may represent the truth to ourselves best by saying that Christ assumed humanity under the conditions of life belonging to man fallen, though not sinful promptings from within." [15] Moffatt, however, thinks that " this is not in the writer's mind at all. He is too eager to enter into any psychological analysis." " To him and his readers Jesus is sinless, not in virtue of a divine prerogative, but as the result of a real human experience which proved successful in the field of temptation." [16] From our point of view both these positions are true. One is a theological deduction from the side of dogmatics. The other is adherence to the stated facts without any attempt to draw theological conclusions. This is to look at the proposition from the angle of Biblical theology.

The realistic portrayal of the human life of Jesus does not stop here; it moves ahead toward a worthy climax. At this stage of the picture the author introduces two concepts — obedience and *archegon*, the perfecter of faith. These two ideas bring into relief the previous part of the story by explicating the meaning of suffering. We discover a new depth in the suffering of Jesus. He is growing into the fullness of ethicospiritual status by undergoing a profound moral and spiritual discipline, and this path lies through the valley of the shadow of death, nay, even death. Secondly, these concepts anticipate the goal. It is the perfecting of the *archegon* — the Leader.

The verse " For it was fitting that He for whom and through whom all things exist, in bringing many sons to glory, should perfect by suffering the Prince Leader of their salvation " (Heb. 2:10) is a befitting introduction to this section. The verse brings out the close relation between creation and redemption. It discloses *doxa* as the common destiny of man. Men can be brought to this *doxa*, which is their salvation, only through the Prince-Leader. This Prince-Leader must be perfect. This can be achieved through suffering. The suffering of Jesus, therefore, is not accidental to God's universe, but necessary.

The kind of life that Jesus led in order to prepare himself for this end can be seen from a high vantage point in his life. " For Jesus during His earthly life offered up prayers and entreaties, crying aloud and weeping as He pleaded with Him who was able to save Him from death, and He was heard for His godly fear." (Heb. 5:7.) The verse covers the whole life of Jesus, and now we see him in the Garden of Gethsemane.

Jesus is face to face with death. In this supreme crisis he surrenders himself to God. The suffering of Jesus at this point is fathomless. The identification with man's fate (and God's will) is so infinitely deep that human imagination is paralyzed in trying to visualize it. The author himself is overwhelmed by what he is struggling to describe. The impact of the historical Jesus is profound. In the midst of this tense atmosphere the author quietly and reverently moves toward the climax. " Although He was God's Son, yet He learned obedience from the sufferings which He endured; and so, having been made perfect, He became to all who obey Him the source and giver of eternal salvation." (Heb. 5:8-9.)

Here the Leader — the *archegon* — is perfected. The path from the sinner in need of salvation to the Savior who gives salvation is made manifest in the life of Jesus. This does not mean that Jesus was a sinner who became Savior. It simply means that in the life of Jesus, so humanly lived, the drama of man's salvation is enacted and completed objectively. It is now for man to avail himself of it. The writer in the above verse also struggles to express a certain organic unity between Jesus as the " Son of God " and the *archegon* who is perfected through obedience. This brings home to us the profound " reality " of Jesus. And this, his being what he is, also discloses the gulf between him and other men. So then he is compelled to say " let us fling aside every encumbrance and the sin that so readily entangles our feet. And let us run, . . . simply fixing our gaze upon Jesus, the Leader and Perfecter of faith " (Heb. 12:1-2).

THE SYNOPTICS

The Synoptics are not biographies in our sense of the word. They are the testimonies of the primitive church to the fact of Jesus Christ. These testimonies, which were first presented to the hearers in oral preaching and teaching, were later committed to writing for use in Christian communities. They therefore are historical but not pure history. They contain something more. It is the witness of faith. Considered as a whole, they are faithful history as well as faith-history. In these accounts one cannot successfully separate faith from history and history from faith. Any such attempt although necessary cannot ultimately succeed.

The Gospels give us a clear-cut picture of Jesus from birth to resurrection and ascension. Mark simply assumes the birth for the purposes of his narrative. Matthew and Luke, however, give us an account of the virgin birth. (Matt. 1:18-25; Luke 2:4-7.) Both the accounts are independent presentations on the basis of a common source. It seems as though both Matthew and Luke were working at their source material at the same time. At least there is not much passage of time; otherwise, it is likely that Luke would have made use of such a formulation.[17]

He is circumcised after eight days and is given the name "Jesus." (Luke 2:21.) The account here evidently lays more emphasis on naming than circumcision. He is then taken to the Temple and presented before the Lord.[18] At the age of twelve the child is seen among the rabbis in the Temple. He is learning by listening as well as by asking and answering questions. At the same time Luke does not fail to mention the growth of the child in stature and in wisdom as well as in favor with God and man. (Luke 2:40; 2:51-52.) He is also obedient to his parents. Luke uses this instance as a literary device to make a transition and relate his adolescence to his ministry. Creed says: "A single incident from the boyhood of Jesus illustrates his 'growth in wisdom' and makes a transition from the infancy to the public ministry. It is in keeping with the psychological and biographical interest of Luke to introduce a link of this kind. Moreover, the story furthers his literary aim of giving a continuous and connected narrative." [19]

The Synoptics bring John the Baptist and Jesus together. John is baptizing at the river Jordan, and Jesus unassumingly comes along with the crowd and is baptized by John.[20] After baptism he is tempted. Mark does not say anything beyond that. But both Matthew and Luke give us the three(?) temp-tations.[21] The temptations are most comprehensive in their nature and scope. These temptations do not by any means signify the end of temptations. He seems to be tempted all the way through his life.

The approximate year for the starting of the work of his ministry is 30. (Luke 3:23.) He went far and wide to deliver his message. He taught and preached while touring around in the villages and towns, in a house, on the mountain, by the lakeside in a boat, and on the road. He proclaimed the gospel of the Kingdom and restored sick and abnormal people of all sorts to normal health. The only condition was their trust in his ability to heal them. He talked and argued with the scribes and the Pharisees. He had gone not only to the Jewish school to which every normal Jewish boy had to go, but he also possessed adequate knowledge of rabbinic Hebrew. No won-der the rabbis also called him "Rabbi." He chose twelve dis-ciples and sent them on the same mission. They came back successful, and he saw through that the defeat of evil forces. They all lived together, wherever they went. After they con-fessed that he was the Christ, he saw in them the continuation of the "remnant." It is this which is the "earnest" of the com-ing of the Kingdom in power.

He is so human that he is thirsty and hungry, tired and re-laxed. He works and rests; sleeps and is awake; weeps and is sorrowful in the sorrow of others; rejoices and is happy in the joy of others. He loves and waits for the return of love. Even if it is not returned, he still loves. His supreme devotion is to the will of the Father. He therefore puts first things first. "Render to Caesar that which is Caesar's and to God that which is God's." The Temple is cleansed because it is God's house where God should be worshiped in the attitude of prayer. It is not a market place. He therefore rides into Jeru-salem. His devotion to the will of the Father and his knowl-edge of the fact that he is the Messiah lead him into open con-flict with the vested religious interests. Seeing that his end is

near, he arranges for a fellowship meal. This meal is an acted
parable, bringing home the reality of the "New Israel," "the
remnant," the "New Humanity." Next, he is seen kneeling
down in the Garden of Gethsemane. He looks broken, as if he
is bearing an infinite burden. His decision is made, and he is
ready for the supreme act. He is betrayed, caught, tried in religious and civil courts. He is given up to be executed. They
nail him to the cross. He dies. The whole drama ends in a defeat. A sense of meaninglessness and frustration seizes those
who had entertained different hopes. But the fact of the resurrection dispels the darkness, and that light discloses the end of
time, the fulfillment of history and existence. The things are
consummated, and he has ascended just as he descended. And
between these two journeys the meaning of existence is fulfilled. That is what made the church and gave it the power
to conquer the powers of evil which drive men to frustration
and to the abyss of meaninglessness.

His teaching is not like that of the rabbis. It is full of authority; people sense it and are amazed. His manner of speech
and delivery is winsome. His words are gracious, and people
admire and applaud him. At the same time there is a certain
severity about him, his teaching puts his hearers on guard,
and they become his enemies. He is the friend of children and
they flock to him, but he is the relentless critic of the false
and of the assumed innocence of the self-righteous scribes and
Pharisees. His method of approach to the Pharisees is controversial, but not with a view to win the argument and lose
the man. To the generality of people he conveys his meaning
in the simple language of nature, of the home, and of the community. And with the disciples he talks the language of intimacy and love.

THE TEACHINGS AND THEIR FORM

The emphasis on the form and content of Jesus' teaching
has shifted from time to time. Under the literalistic interpretation the form and content were so confused that they both

became infallible. Under the influence of liberal thought the content was divorced from its form. And all that we had was a sum total of general timeless and colorless principles. Under the critical and historical method we arrived at a differentiation between form and content. But inasmuch as the method became purely critical and historical, the forms became too rigid and dictatorial for their content. They spatialized and temporalized the content entirely. In the teaching of Jesus, however, both have their rightful place. The distinction between them is not premeditated, and the harmony between them is instinctive and spontaneous.

On the whole, the teachings of Jesus have been more emphasized, and rightly so, but the result has been that the form in which they were presented has been ignored more than often. Goguel says: "Of the teaching of Jesus it may be said that the wealth of its content has caused the originality of the form to be ignored. Attention has been concentrated, but this means that very often the way in which they were said was overlooked more than was just or right. The words and discourses of Jesus, however, would bear comparison with the most finished products of the human mind and ought to be ranked among the masterpieces of world literature." [22] Of all our Gospel sources it is to L that we are indebted for preserving for us the charm of Jesus' manner. "And they all spoke well of Him, wondering at the words of grace which fell from His lips, while they asked one another, 'Is not this Joseph's son?'" [23] Montefiore commenting on this says: "The audience is not only said to be astonished as in Mark, but even delighted. They admire the beauty of his words." [24] They openly acknowledge the excellence and charm of his eloquence. Along with this formal aspect Montefiore suggests that there may be another view, "that the men of Nazareth are compelled to recognize the power and beauty of the teaching and personality but no sooner do they feel this than they react and rebel against the feeling." [25] To us it appears that both these views are correct but not regarding one and the same verse. The verse under discussion is, however, open to ambiguous interpretation.

Both the above-mentioned views are true if we keep in mind the verses that follow in the immediate context dealing with the rejection and expelling of Jesus out of the synagogue. John Wick Bowman holds that the dubious interpretation is the result of understanding " gracious words " to mean " words regarding the saving grace of God." " That Luke does not mean this is proved by two observations: First, that the comment was made by the people at the beginning, rather than at the end, of the discourse. . . . Again, when in fact that day at Nazareth they had listened long enough to discover the content of his message they became so enraged at it that, despite his pleasing manner, they rose up and threw him out! " [26] Even at this time when the mob was hysterical and was determined to throw him down headlong from that high hill, he manifests graciousness which is so majestic that it entirely disarms the crowd. Otto Borchert, referring to this incident, says: " Up till then Jesus had allowed himself to be pushed and hustled, but at the critical moment it seemed to us he suddenly grew in stature. Thus he strode through the excited crowd, every inch a king." [27] To this should also be added his wide popularity with the crowds and the fierce hostility directed at him from the religious hierarchy.

These descriptions lead us to believe that Jesus was an extraordinarily strong personality. Wherever he went and wherever his message was heard people either followed him as disciples or laid plans to do away with him. This brings into high relief both the graciousness and the sternness of Jesus. His graciousness is the instrument of the saving grace. This saving grace if not accepted assumes the sternness of the death knell for the rejector.

A very tender instance of his graciousness is found in the way he attracts children. They come and gather round him. Though this is far removed from formal apologetics, it is certain evidence of his winsome and gracious personality.

The beauty of the words of our Lord immediately implies

their form and structure. Here we will follow the lead of the late C. F. Burney.[28] Jesus uses nearly all the devices used in Hebrew poetry. There is one all-inclusive word, " parallelism," under which all these devices can be summed up. Bishop Lowth uses this term and defines it thus: "The correspondence of one verse, or line, with another, I call parallelism. When a proposition is delivered and a second is subjoined to it, or drawn under it, equivalent or contrasted with it, in sense; or similar to it in the form of grammatical construction; these I call parallel lines; and the words or phrases, answering one to another in the corresponding lines, parallel terms. Parallel lines may be reduced to three sorts: parallel synonyms, parallels antithetic, and parallels synthetic." [29] To this Burney adds a fourth, called step parallelism or climactic parallelism: [30] the significant thing in it is recapitulation which adds definiteness to the recorded sayings. T. W. Manson suggests another, which in his opinion has not previously been taken into consideration. It is " compound parallelism," and is found in the words of Jesus. " Here the parallelism covers not single clauses containing each one simple idea, but still larger aggregates each of which contains many clauses." [31]

There are three types of rhythm in Hebrew poetry: (1) four-beat, (2) three-beat, and (3) *kena*-rhythm or dirge. The major difficulty of detecting rhythm in the Gospels is that the Gospels are " translations," and the translators evidently made no effort to preserve the rhythm of Jesus' sayings. However, we are not without evidence, " since parallelism, being inherent in the form and substance of the saying, is as apparent in translation as in the original language of the speaker." [32] Rhythm was not accidental to his teaching. It is likely that he employed four-beat rhythm to instruct his followers.[33]

Rhyme is another device that Jesus employs. This is not a special mark of literary Hebrew poetry. " There is, however, a class of ancient Hebrew poetry in which the use of rhyme was probably a favorite device, namely, the popular poetry of the relatively uncultured." [34] In popular folk poetry and teaching,

rhyme is used on purpose. Burney also inclines to think "that
when rhyme occurs in the Lord's parallelistic teaching, it is
equally done to design, and was adopted as likely to aid the
memory of his hearers." [35]

Whereas it is clear now that Jesus uses all the literary devices
employed in Hebrew poetry, yet the antithetic parallelism is
most characteristic of him. T. W. Manson writes that this
strophic parallelism is Jesus' "special contribution to the forms
of poetry in general." [36]

In the teaching of Jesus nothing is more outstanding than
the use of parables. In these parables are conveyed great truths
regarding God and human destiny. Just as the other poetical
forms disclose a single mind at work, so also the parables disclose, "taken as a whole, the stamp of a highly individual
mind." [37]

It is necessary to distinguish between allegory and parable
because the interpretation of the parable has suffered a great
deal at the hands of allegorical interpretation. It is true that
the Gospels do give a little support to such a method, but on the
whole such a view cannot be supported by the nature of
the parable. Bishop Lowth gives a criterion of the parable,
"namely, that it be consistent throughout, and that the literal
be never confounded with the figurative sense." [38] "The typical
parable," says Dodd, "presents one single point of comparison.
The details are not intended to have independent significance.
In an allegory, on the other hand, each detail is a separate
metaphor, with a significance of its own." [39] The parables are
not tales told to bring out certain moral lessons. They are
drawn from concrete life situations and are therefore conditioned; yet they are not exhausted by the relativities of life from
which they are drawn because they bring to bear on our life
circumstances the fact of the eternal — the ever contemporary.[40]
They are artistic, historical, and concrete, and portray the
relevance of the will and purpose of God for human nature
and destiny. Their purpose is to bring people to faith through
repentance. T. W. Manson divides the parables into three

classes: (1) those by which appeal is made to the conscience of man; (2) those which portray a principle of the providence of God; and (3) those which include both these purposes. The first two are the main types. He says: "They present either a type of human conduct or a principle of God's government of the world. In the former case the primary appeal is to the conscience, in the latter to the religious insight and faith of the hearers. In some cases both features are present in the same parable, though even in these cases one side is usually predominant." [41]

The effectiveness of the parable does not consist of the way and of the spirit in which the speaker presents it. That element is there. But its true effectiveness lies in the response of the hearers. It may be that Mark 4:11-12 can be understood from this point of view. If the hearers are indifferent and cold, the parables would not have any meaning for them. But, on the other hand, those which respond with faith and insight see that they portray the Kingdom of God in their midst. Manson very rightly says it is "clear that the purpose of parables is not to harden the hearts of the hearers, but that it is the hardness of the heart of the hearers that defeats the purpose of the parables." [42]

His Authority and Wisdom

The teaching of Jesus is characterized by the unique and novel element of authority.[43] This serves as the line of demarcation for the common people between him and the rabbis. The people are awe-inspired because the like of him they have never heard and seen. This authority of Jesus, which Bowman calls his "ethical Lordship," is derived through his filial relationship of love and intimacy of knowledge with his Father. In Mark 6:2, people are described as marveling at the wisdom of Jesus. Bowman sees the relation between authority and wisdom the same as that between form and content. This authoritative spiritual insight is what marks him as quite unique from the rabbis. "It was, as we are persuaded, this inner compelling power, an ethicospiritual earnestness and depth," says Bowman, "which the commonality of men recognized in Jesus' teaching as unique." [44] This is what constituted the challenge for men and violently divided men either in favor of or against him. His authority was the authority of God, and the sharpness of his insight was like the double-edged sword.

BAPTISM, TEMPTATION, AND GETHSEMANE

We have already dealt with the baptism, and here we will try to mention only those things which have not been included in the previous treatment. It is hard to guess the religious experience of our Lord before the baptism. But if the baptism be regarded as the coronation ceremony, it becomes clear that the underlying foundation of Jesus' religious experience was loyalty to the will of his Father. Both the baptism and the temptation confront him with two alternatives. On the one hand is the will of God, and on the other hand the will of Satan. His baptism and temptation both mark him out as the Son of God. He would do his Father's will at all cost.

Manson and Bowman both agree that Jesus was presented with alternatives. [45] Bowman, however, pursues this line of argument in detail. He believes that before Jesus came for baptism, his mind was made up in favor of the Kingdom of God over against the kingdom of Satan. The word *shub*, together with its richer Greek translation *metanoein*, primarily means to make a choice or decision between alternatives. Once a person has chosen to be on the side of God, his sinfulness is judged accordingly. In the case of Jesus, as far as evidence goes, there was no sinfulness to confess. His baptism coming after this decision, the descent of the Spirit upon him is therefore nothing but the autograph of God the Father — the heavenly "Voice" confirming the call of the prophetic voice that he is the Messiah.

Now it is quite natural, nay, inevitable that such a one should be tempted with all the cunning and subtlety of the forces of evil. Can the sinful order of the world leave one that ultimately means its destruction unmolested? This indeed is impossible. That is why after the baptism there is the temptation. The two are related by the existing constitution of the forces of evil. It seems to us right to proceed on the assumption that all these temptations attack from one angle or the other the central decision of Jesus: his decision to do the will of his Father.

The first temptation would be to induce him to use miraculous power to achieve his end. He is tempted to use short cuts and the way of least resistance to fulfill his Messianic vocation. It is an attempt designed to change the entire course of the life of Jesus.

The second temptation is designed to make him tempt God. The temptation implies that, since he is the Son of God, God would take care of him; as a matter of fact, he will have to take care of him inasmuch as the Son is bound to the Father by necessary relationship. And it does not matter whether the Son behaves this way or that way. The particular instance is to induce action.

The third temptation aims at the reversal of loyalties. It tempts him to obey the evil one rather than God.

These temptations prove that Jesus was conscious of his being the Messiah. He knew that the part of the Messiah entailed humiliation and suffering. The knowledge of this would not deter him from fulfilling his Father's will even if it meant death.

GETHSEMANE

This directly leads us to Gethsemane and is a commentary on what had happened from baptism till then. His manner in Gethsemane is such that we are at once made conscious that he is being sorely tried. The temptation is so strong that under its pressure he is almost broken down. He is heavy in heart and earnest in spirit. Never was such a phenomenon witnessed before, and, from what we know of it, it will not be witnessed again. The cost was weighed, and the decision was made. "Not my will but thy will be done." When he was downcast he seemed to be bearing an infinite burden, but when he rose up one could unmistakably behold the opening up of such fathomless depths of compassion that even an infinity of worlds would not be able to set a limit to it. The Father was the ultimate reality of his being, and the Son identified himself with this reality to the last limits of love and surrender. That is why the cross stands next to Gethsemane.

THE CROSS

The cross is the symbol of what God can do and also of what man can do. The cross shows that, if God comes to man, it means his salvation. But it also discloses the kind of hospitality men are able to provide for him. They crucify him. The cross is the symbol of eternity in the midst of history, but it also signifies the unconcealed rejection of eternity by history. It symbolized God's love for man, but at the same time it portrays man's hatred for God. Man and historical forces hate the cross and reject it because it means the destruction of man and history as they are. They did not crucify him blindly but in full knowledge of the fact that his acceptance meant the destruction of their *status quo*. The sting lies in the fact that they did not know that even his crucifixion would mean the end of their ways and their days. It is probably this that Jesus had in mind when he said, " Father, forgive them, for they know not what they do." Viewed from the side of God it is the symbol of " It is finished," but from the man's side it is meaninglessness and defeat.

The cross is a paradox, nay, it is the supreme paradox; and in this paradox lies the salvation as well as the death of man, of history, and of existence.

THE FOURTH GOSPEL

The Gospel According to John is a thoroughgoing example of faith-history. Its being faith-history has constituted a great stumbling block for scholars. Those who have tried to disentangle the witness of faith from history have regarded it a pattern of higher generalities. The Gospel in the hands of such critics became an esoteric book or a treatise on metaphysical philosophy. Those who tried to separate history from the witness of faith explained away the things that a scientific historian by virtue of his task and profession is unable to see and account for. Both attempts have resulted in bad allegory and bad history. This happened for the simple reason that allegory could not allegorize all the tough material and history could not reduce the witness of faith to mere phenomenology. The Gospel is faith-history, and that is how it is to be understood. Its literary unity does not give freedom to the critic to experiment with it with the dissecting tools of his critical apparatus. This Gospel is history as well as interpretation, and it is impossible to drive a wedge between the two.[46] The unity is so finely wrought out that the line of demarcation is not visible. This invisibility is a sign to the experimenting temper that the material is dangerous.

The problem of the chronology of the life events of Jesus has led the critics to doubt the historical character of the Gospel. There is no doubt that the Evangelist has handled his material in a free and nonchronological way; but to say that he is purely ideational and unhistorical is to misunderstand the aim and the theme of the Gospel. The Gospel is nonchronological, but that does not mean that it is unchronological. If one assumed it so, one would be rudely shocked to find that the "mystical" Evangelist presents hard facts of history and realistic topography.

The Evangelist is indeed historical. He is historical in the ultimate sense of the term. He raises the problem of the meaning of history. This he does by presenting the nonhistorical in the midst of history. This, says Edwyn Hoskyns, is "the Problem of all problems, for it is concerned with the relation between time and eternity, between what is finite and what is infinite, between phenomena and reality, in fact between man and God." [47] The Evangelist does not raise the question of the meaning of history by resorting to history as such. He bears witness to

the eternal and nonhistorical, to the Word of God, in the life history of Jesus of Nazareth. The Evangelist then places this Jesus
in the stream of immediate and universal history, thereby giving
rise to "the Problem of all problems." History could not exhaust
the history of Jesus and make him purely the Jesus of history —
his life gives meaning to all history. Therefore Hoskyns says:
"From so grave a misunderstanding of the Jesus of history, and
of the tradition, oral and written, of His life, the author of the
Fourth Gospel determines to rescue his readers. But he will not
do this by throwing the Jesus of history to the winds — that is
proving disastrous — but by insisting that the tradition itself has
a meaning peering out of it at every point, a meaning which is
'beyond history,' and which alone makes sense of history. To disclose this underlying meaning of the tradition he wrote his
Gospel." [48]

John Knox in his little book *The Man Christ Jesus* has voiced
a criticism that the Fourth Evangelist underrates the humanity
of Jesus.[49] This he does over against Paul. But in all probability
his question remains the same even if Paul is not brought into
the picture. We are inclined to feel that the Evangelist may not
give so much material, but whatever he gives leaves us in no
doubt about the humanity of Jesus. We should mention another thing before we pass on to the humanity of Jesus in the
Fourth Gospel. Wherever mention is made of the human traits
of Jesus, the Evangelist also mentions the divine side. This
may lead the reader to believe that the Evangelist only wants
to emphasize the latter. But it is the Evangelist's way of saying
things. He mentions both the human and the divine as pertaining to one person. Strachan says that the Evangelist qualified
"his [Jesus'] emphasis on the humanity of Jesus by emphasizing equally his divinity. There is no elaborate logical reflection.
The two aspects of his personality — human and divine are
naïvely set side by side. This is in accordance with the whole
conception of the person of Jesus in this Gospel." [50]

Let us examine then how Jesus is really man. The Evangelist
says, "And the Word became flesh, and lived awhile in our

midst, so that we saw His glory." The Word became flesh means that the Word became man. The writer is not trying to describe the process of how the Word became flesh. He is making a judgment of faith which is at the same time a historical judgment. This is further sustained by his living among men like a man. He is no apparition. He is not God masquerading in human guise. He is exposed to the experience and perception of the external senses. The word "saw" in the above context and the "heard" and "handled" of I John are very significant. He is truly flesh and blood as far as human senses can feel and describe. The humanity rather than the divinity of Jesus is here emphasized. This becomes all the more important when we realize that Docetism was abroad trying to cramp the Christian movement.

He is baptized by John, although the descent of the dove is more significant here than the baptism. It is revealed that John did not know Jesus. But when this is said it means that John did not know Jesus in a profound and significant way. The ordinary acquaintance is not by this fact set aside.

The topography of the Evangelist is different, and Jesus is seen spending most of his time in and around Jerusalem. He teaches in the Temple. On his way to Galilee being tired and thirsty, he sits down to rest at the well of Jacob. He converses with the woman of Samaria while his disciples go into town to buy some provisions. A little later at the invitation of the Samaritans he stayed with them for two days.

Jesus, seeing an immense crowd coming toward him, said to Philip, "Where shall we buy bread for all these people to eat?" This question shows Jesus' limitation of knowledge, although the Evangelist according to his fashion rejoins that, "He said this to put Philip to the test, for He Himself knew what He was going to do."

The Evangelist mentions Jesus' affection for Martha, Mary, and Lazarus. And when Jesus came to see the dead Lazarus, finding Mary and the Jews who were with her wailing and weeping, "Jesus, in indignation and deeply troubled, asked them, 'Where have you laid him?' 'Master, come and see,' was their reply. Jesus burst into tears." Was there any truer affection than this to be found anywhere? How tender and how human!

Jesus eats the meal of fellowship with his disciples and then washes their feet. Some regard this as the sign of Jesus' humility, and others as condescension. Both of these are apt to minimize the humanity of Jesus. The real significance of it is that it depicts the death and the humiliation of Jesus. This brought his future suffering into bold relief, but they could not understand this meaning. It meant also that they, his disciples, would also pass through death and humiliation.[51]

The last human touch is the entrusting of his mother to the "beloved disciple." It is capable of high symbolic interpretation, but in its concreteness and individuality it portrays his pathos and sense of human relationship.

"The real human personality of Jesus is the spearhead of the Evangelist's message. Jesus is a divine being who has become truly man, the Logos made flesh. The portrait of Jesus in this Gospel is a theological interpretation of the human life, based on actual traditions of the life and ministry of Jesus."[52]

RECONSTRUCTION OF THE NEW TESTAMENT CHRISTOLOGY: THE HUMANITY

Did the Christian community create Jesus Christ or did he create it? is a persistent question. It means two things. In the first place it means that Jesus Christ is the creation of the Christian mind; secondly, that Jesus Christ is a historical person, but the significance that is attributed to him is a figment of pious imagination. The historical view of the life and meaning of Jesus has been both held and defended in and outside of the Christian church — that it does not matter who he was and under what circumstances he grew up; all that matters is the timeless teachings bequeathed to us from the past. It is true that in the highly generalized form of the teaching, the historicity and the individuality of the person are at the point of being lost. These teachings can be affixed or suffixed to any name historical or imaginary. Modern Biblical scholarship does not put much premium on this objection. The historical is no problem for us any more. The second meaning of this objection, however, is more relevant to our task. It was vigorously defended in Germany and found many followers abroad. The trend of modern scholarship, to a fair extent, has taken the sting out of this objection also. He was not made Messiah by his followers; but was conscious of it in his lifetime and came to regard himself in the deepest possible way the Messiah who is the Suffering Servant of God and the exalted Son of Man.[53]

It must, however, be confessed that whenever we grapple with the fact of Jesus Christ, the question raised above will undoubtedly be raised again. And we will have to rethink the answer in our own way. The nature of his personality is such that one cannot help asking, Is this a real or unreal person?

The New Testament, as we have studied it, presents two aspects. It affirms that Jesus Christ is a historical person. This the writers do not present according to the wishes of a modern scientific historian, but they provide necessary historical data which confirm the historicity of Jesus beyond a shadow of doubt. But they go farther than this. They are not interested in the presentation of a historical person. They are selective, and they choose to present a particular person. They do so by unanimously affirming certain things about him. The way they present him also brings out his singularity. The examination of the form and teaching of Jesus establishes the fact that a single original mind is at work. Rabbi Klausner has said that all the teachings of Jesus item by item can be duplicated from Jewish sources. Students of other religions may say, and they do say, that all religions are essentially one. It may be said here that since the teaching can be so duplicated from the universal fund of religious literature that those who give it a particular form can be dispensed with. People who have made such assertions, however, have to a greater or lesser degree realized that the phenomenon confronting them in the teaching

of Jesus is relatively different from others. This difference they
elucidate by pointing out that in the teaching of Jesus there
exists a greater and therefore relatively unique degree of concentration. The teachings are set forth in a more concentrated
way than the corresponding teachings of the Jewish rabbis
were. This constitutes, according to them, the originality of
Jesus. The New Testament writers, in presenting Christ the
way they do, realize the force of this argument and admit its
truth, but they seem to go beyond this. As a matter of fact,
their interest is not in what he says but in what he is. They are
interested in his words and acts as aspects of his person. This
means clearly that they are more concerned with the person
than the teachings. The principle that emerges is this, that in
their minds they could not separate the person from the teaching. The teaching is important, but the most important thing
is the person. It is here that the New Testament writers differ
from anyone attempting to drive a wedge between his teaching
and the person. Their opponents exalt the teaching and lower
the person. They exalt the person without lowering the teaching, and at the same time make it clear where their emphasis
lies.

A question needs to be asked at this point. What do they
affirm of this man Christ Jesus? They affirm that he is a man
like any other man. He is tempted and tried in all possible
ways. He accepts living under human limitations, even under
the condition of human sin. They lived with him, and they saw,
handled, and heard him as truly as they did themselves and
their friends. He grows up and fulfills the requirements of the
Law. He works and is tired, hungry, and thirsty. He loves his
relatives and friends. He can be angry and has enemies and
persecutors. He understands human nature and its problems.
He is ready to forgive. He is the lover of the world of nature.
But in his actions, speech, and daily contacts he lays bare a
secret. In his prayers he pours out his soul to God. He manifests deep affection and unflinching obedience to someone else,
whom he addresses as his Father. This seems to be the funda-

mental reality of his being. And it is his Father's will and purpose that he seeks to fulfill, and his Kingdom that he seeks to bring about. His charismatic activity and life is devoted to them. He and his Father are one, and it is in obedience to his will that he mounts the cross. His manner of speech is gracious, and children and grownups flock around him. But his speech is not ordinary speech. It is full of authority and of wisdom such as has never been witnessed before. He is unique among men and his like is not to be seen. His disciples realize that he is the Christ. Through and in his humanity they catch a glimpse of something greater than itself. They wonder and marvel but remain confused till the resurrection opens their eyes and the Holy Spirit brings home the full truth.

They affirm also that he is Rabbi, Prophet, High Priest, Son of Man, Son of God, Logos, and Lord. How can they affirm these things of one and the same person? Such a mosaic of attributes can only be the creation of a fanciful mind. One person cannot be all these things. Such thoughts are no doubt stirred in our minds when we see this composite picture of Christ. The writers do not relate all these qualities in a single unified whole. They affirm these of one living person. This they do because their knowledge of him has steadily increased and they have come to know him better. But what they affirmed of him at an earlier stage does not stand in contradiction to what they affirm of him later. This is also due to the fact that they are in touch with a many-sided person. And, although it is the same person who comes into contact with them at both earlier or later stages, the implications of the manifold personality do not become evident all of a sudden. They demand maturity of discernment. Yet another factor enters in also. Jesus was a growing person, and he underwent moral and spiritual growth as truly as he did physical. His disciples mention the fact of his growth but maintain a strange silence on his inner development. They seem to regard him as statically perfect. This fact might have hindered as well as helped their appreciation of Jesus.

This phenomenon of their description bears witness to two factors. Firstly, their inability to describe and evaluate him adequately. Secondly, their concern to portray him as well as they can. This they find they cannot do by simply resorting to human categories. There is a certain uniqueness attached to his humanity which human terms and their breadth of meaning cannot describe. They leave it at that. It is only after the resurrection experience and the descent of the Holy Spirit that they are enabled with a clearer conviction to give a name to that uniqueness. This they try to express by the terms " Son of Man," " Son of God," " the Logos," or " the Lord." It is because of the humanity of Jesus Christ that Paul is able to call him " the Lord," " the heavenly man," and " the quickening Spirit." It is because of the " Logos become flesh," who tabernacled in our midst, that John is able to say, " And we beheld his glory, the glory as of the only begotten of the Father, full of grace and truth," and that " In the beginning was the Logos, and the Logos was with God and the Logos was God." Because of his suffering on the cross and the resurrection the Synoptists affirm that he is the " Suffering Servant " and the exalted " Son of Man." His sacrifice leads the author of Hebrews to say that he had offered himself before God " through the eternal Spirit."

Humanity here is not used as a means to an end. Nor is it deified so that the erstwhile man has become God. They have borne faithful witness to what they saw. And what they saw and experienced was that this man was not merely man. He is the God-Man. They declare it; they do not prove it.

IV

JESUS CHRIST

Let the very spirit which was in Christ Jesus be in you also. From the beginning He had the nature of God. Yet He did not regard equality with God as something at which He should grasp. Nay, He stripped Himself of His glory, and took on Him the nature of a bondservant by becoming a man like other men. And being recognized as truly human, He humbled Himself and even stooped to die; and that too a death on the cross. It is because of this also that God has so highly exalted Him, and has conferred on Him the Name which is supreme above every other name, in order that in the Name of Jesus every knee should bow, of beings in the highest heavens, of those on the earth, and of those in the underworld, and that every tongue should confess that Jesus Christ is Lord, to the glory of God the Father. (Phil. 2:6-11.)

I hazard the prophecy that that religion will conquer which can render to popular understanding some eternal greatness incarnate in the passage of temporal fact. (*Adventure of Ideas*, by A. N. Whitehead, p. 41.)

Both philosophy and theology should start neither with God nor with man (for there is no bridge between these two principles), but rather with the God-Man. (*Freedom and the Spirit*, by Nicolas Berdyaev, p. 189.)

101

The Problem

JESUS CHRIST is not someone who can be safely ignored. He is unique, and every age and every generation has to reckon with him. He confronts everyone; yet no age has been able to settle entirely the questions and problems that have been raised by him. Men have tried to evaluate him according to the needs and knowledge of their time. Such attempts have existed for two thousand years. None of them have been adequate enough to settle the question for good. Indeed most of them have labored at explaining away one element or the other to which their portrait of Jesus Christ could not do justice. We do not imply that they did it consciously, but wherever the motive has been the presentation of Jesus Christ according to the canons of logical consistency, one aspect or another of his life has either been ignored, underestimated, or explained away. This, however, does not plead for presenting the whole, with utter disregard for consistency, as a general principle of interpretation. It may be that when we endeavor to present Jesus Christ according to the intention of the New Testament, in terms of our rational and systematic categories, we lose something and fail to present the whole. The modern portrait of Jesus Christ, as any other, should be in accordance with the New Testament irrespective of the means and tools of presentation. But since every generation of men has to discover the Christ for itself, no amount of beating the air would facilitate its task; for it will have to go to the New Testament. What is then, in brief, the New Testament picture of the Christ, as we have studied it?

The New Testament Picture

The New Testament picture has two sides — one divine and the other human. In the divine side it is affirmed of him that he was existent before everything else. He is the effulgence of God's glory and the express image of his character. He is the Christ, the Lord of Glory, and the quickening Spirit. He is the

Logos become flesh, who tabernacled in our midst, and we beheld his glory as the only begotten of the Father full of grace and truth.

On the other hand he is weak, dependent, needy, tired, hungry, and thirsty, as any other man. He rejoices with those who rejoice but also shares the sorrow of those who weep. He has limitations and fulfills the requirements of the Law. His temptations are real and as wide in scope as can be imagined. He prays with rare earnestness, and, in spite of living under the condition of human sin, does not succumb to it. His life is dedicated to the fulfillment of the will of God, whom he calls his Father. He grows in knowledge and in favor with him and with men.

To put it figuratively, there is a twofold movement in the New Testament, of which Jesus Christ is the meeting point. One is God-manward movement, and it implies the coming of God in our midst — the Emmanuel and the Word become flesh. The other is a man-Godward movement, implying that in Christ is summed up everything, and he is subjected to God so that God be all in all.

THE TASK

The task is to preserve these two aspects without doing injustice to either. Our task would be easy if we undertook to paint the picture from one angle or the other. From the divine side the coming of God in the midst of men would mean that God uses humanity only as a means of facilitating his stay here. He indeed would be masquerading in human form. Humanity would be pushed to the periphery or explained away, and God would be an apparition. But this at least makes sense, in so far as it is a logical whole. It is true when measured by rational consistency. Incarnation in this sense would be some species of theophany.

From the human angle the moral and spiritual growth of the man Jesus would be such that at some one time there would be perfect attunement between his will and God's. So much so that he would have become divine. Divinity in this context is an appendage to humanity, and the result is some sort of deification of the man Jesus. This also makes sense, because it submits perfectly to the way of discursive and horizontal thinking.

Both of these approaches, logical though they are, create a system but lose the person. The task consists in retaining the person, which implies the safeguarding of the two sides of his personality. Again, if we could get away by simply affirming these two sides of one person — Jesus Christ — our task would be fairly easy. But the demands of our age are such that we cannot simply affirm: we have to explain.

Now it is clear that the New Testament writers did not do the explaining, in our sense of the term. They affirmed and bore witness — which, no doubt, involved a certain amount of interpretation. But they interpret it only to this extent, that they bore witness to the person and what that person had done to and for them. They did not, however, set out to explain the content of their experience. We immediately begin to see the difference when we move out of the first century into the second, the third, the fourth, and so on. We realize that the experience of Jesus Christ is necessary for us, without forgetting at the same time that our task is much more complicated than that of the first-century Christians. They set no precedent in systematic delineation which we can copy or follow. The impact of the Master's personality was so vital and thorough that intellectual inconsistencies were not felt; the person solved for them what we set about to do with our puny systems.

The church at Chalcedon provided us with a formula. It is in keeping with the New Testament insight. But it is also an affirmation. The church simply stated its belief. We are grateful for the statement, for it defines the boundary of theological operation with reference to the Christ, but it does not help us in our task of intelligible presentation. But is it necessary that we should do the explaining? Why should truth be apologetic? Some of our number think that we should simply declare and positively affirm. They may be right, but it is certain that they hold to a half-truth. Truth needs to be propagated, and the truth is served if it can be presented according to the needs and apprehension of the recipients. This by no means implies the attenuation of the truth. When we have to relate the truth to life and its problems an intelligible explanation is necessary in so far as it is possible. Biblical theology, in the strict sense of the term, is not adequate to the needs of our time. It gives the raw material for systematic theology whereby the Biblical message can be intelligently and methodically communicated to the world. Systematic theology is, however, not the last word in logical presentation. If systematic theology assumes that it can unravel the enigma of the Christ by having recourse to discursive reason, it is entirely mistaken. And in the event of such an enterprise it proves itself a science of dubious value. We cannot discuss this matter here at any length. Suffice it to say for the present that we do not underrate reason. The elemental fact is that reason necessarily plays a secondary role in the Christological context. The fact of the Christ is given, and reason does not create it. Reason, therefore, if it has to function here, can function only by recognizing the limitations imposed on it by the primary given fact.

But what is the use of launching forth on an enterprise which is condemned to failure before it is undertaken? It is true that we do not presume to solve the problem undertaken, and it is also probable that, in so far as we remain what we are, this problem may never be solved. After this is said, there still remains enough justification for pursuing the task. First, in the event of abandoning the task, one would be confronted by so much inertia that one might as well be doing something that has important bearing on life rather than sit and decay. Secondly, by the same logic we should commit suicide rather than live, for we cannot solve the ultimate problems of life. Thirdly, it is only by trying that we can hope to get an insight into reality. And by contributing this to the insights of others, we with others may be granted a vision of the Christ, even though a dim one. Finally, the New Testament writers have not left us entirely in the dark. They give us a method by which we may be able to scale the heights. This method or theologizing tendency is present in nearly all the writers of the New Testament that we have discussed. In some it is more obvious than in the others. Let us see what this method is.

The Method

The method of these writers is neither conscious nor simple. It is not simply one of deduction or induction. The method would be fairly simple and easy to follow if it stemmed out either from a purely objective, a priori, axiomatic base or from a subjective, a posteriori, and empirical one. The first approach would provide an objective basis or universal axioms for the portrayal of the Christ. The task is like that of an architect who on the basis of his preconceived plan builds a structure. This may carry out all the marks of objectivity and rational validity, but at the best would be a construction, however structural and harmonious.

The second approach would make room for psychological projection of one form or another. It would be empirical, derived from the facts of experience, but at best it would be a concoction of our feeling and imagination. It would not have any foundation other than our own experience, but by laws of empirical measurement and evaluation it may be sound and valid.

These two methods without any relation to each other are mere abstractions, and when the world of our knowledge and experience is investigated under conditioned circumstances they are valid. But when an attempt is made to catch a glimpse of the oneness of the world they are useless tools. Similarly various types of critical studies of the Bible may find, as they have already found, that one or the other method is for them the more convenient. But in order to capture in a synoptic vision the unity of the Bible these tools as such should be left behind in the laboratory. This is most true when we come to the apprehension of the Person of Jesus Christ. The two methods would either pull apart, or merely reduce to one side, the whole Person of the Christ. The New Testament writers, in our judgment, do not use these methods in isolation. Somehow or other in their apprehension of Jesus Christ both these methods are used as one method. They are related, without any touch of artificiality.

This intuitive grasp which enables the New Testament writers to appreciate the unity of the Person of Christ is objective-subjective at the same time. But before giving it out as our method two modifications of it are necessary. First, the objective link of the objective-subjective approach should not be considered as merely " out there." It is " out there " and " over against " us, but it is not static, it is dynamic and active. This object really acts like a subject, and from the point of view of truth it should be subject, needing a subject approach. Second, " subjective " here does not mean divorced from the reality of the divine Subject; it means the experient in relation to the Subject in experience. The other methods followed in isolation would give us neat systems, but the person would be lost. This method has the prospect of retaining the person for us and giving a coherent view of him as far as it is possible. The advantage is gained not at the cost of irrationalism but by giving full credit to reason in all its places of operation. The New Testament writers show by this approach that their experience is real; but it is not limited by them, it is not their creation. They are in relation to a Being over against them from whom through intimate fellowship they have derived this experience. Experience and reality are not separate; they are intimately related in the act of experience, the constituent elements of which are give-and-take, disclosing the two in relation.

THE STARTING POINT: THE RESURRECTION

With this method in hand, the resurrection seems to be the best perspective for the evaluation of Jesus Christ. The New Testament writers, likewise, preach and write about him after

Easter. It is only when the resurrection clarified matters for them and the Holy Spirit provided insight into the mystery that these men began to speak of him confidently and dauntlessly. This, however, does not dispute the fact that the post-resurrection preaching and writing of these men contained information and experience of the pre-resurrection Jesus. The resurrection is not an isolated event in the mind and thinking of the Evangelists. It is very intimately related to their previous experience. The resurrection shows superbly what they had been groping after. Now, these men have faith which cannot be shattered. To them Jesus is the Christ, the Lord of glory. So it is only by reading back from the high vantage point of the resurrection that we can see, as far as it is possible, the totality of the life of Jesus Christ. An evaluation from the birth up to the death does not see the total picture. It only sees one side, but one side seen adequately does not mean the seeing of the whole. Moreover, the Evangelists, though they write and preach from a particular point of view, nevertheless see the Christ through the eyes of the resurrection. From the birth up to the death we see only the growth of the human and not the interrelation of the divine and the human. Our preoccupation is so much with the human that the divine becomes merely an inference.

But looking from the resurrection point does not mean that we plead for starting with the divine. That would be equally one-sided. What the resurrection discloses is neither God as such, nor man as such: it discloses the God-Man. Therefore in the evaluation of the Christ we start neither from man nor from God. These two starting points are not at our disposal. We do not have God as such. He is the God of the world and of man. He is related to his creation. It is the God we deal with and come in contact with, but God as such we never know. So also we do not know man as such. He is an abstraction. The man of our acquaintance is the man in relation. He is an evaluated person. He is either the bondservant of sin and the world, or the bondservant of Christ and the free man of the world. The resurrection rightly and truly presents the God-Man, man the quickening Spirit; Jesus, the Christ and Lord. It is clear, then, that mere categories of divinity and humanity can neither create nor evaluate Christ the God-Man. He is in a category of his own and can be understood only when taken as a unitary being. This is not to deny that both divine and human categories anticipate Christ the God-Man, but it is equally true that no human categories can create the Christ. On the other hand given the God-Man we begin to understand both God and Man.

But how can one understand the Christ from this perspective? We shall have the chance to take up this question a little later. It is, however, necessary to say that it is only the Christian who can understand the Christ in this way. This may sound ridiculous to some, but a glance at the experience of the New Testament writers should bring home the truth. In order to understand the resurrection of Jesus one has to be crucified, buried, and resurrected with him. The implication of the Kingdom in our midst and the experience and foretaste of eternal life here and now, in space time, means that the resurrection is a reality to him who has passed from death into life. The resurrection is basic to such an experience; just as our dual citizenship, i.e., our participation in eternal life while we are still bound by historical temporality, shows the interrelation of the eternal and temporal realms, so also, and far more basically, the resurrection is the meeting ground between time and eternity, and between man and God. The resurrection has an aspect of eternity, but it is not bounded by it. Similarly, it has an aspect of time but is not circumscribed by it. It is on the border line, nay, it *is* the border line, between time and eternity, man and God. The resurrection is historical because it engenders power in history which changes the lives of men and women. It brings into existence historical institutions. But above all, it creates within history a spiritual communion or a fellowship which is the " earnest " of eternity. On the other hand, because the power of the resurrection is not the power of history but of God, the resurrection has an aspect of eternity. The resurrection by presenting Christ the God-Man as a unitary being also shows his relation to God and man. The God-Man with respect to God is very God of very God and in relation to man he is very man of very man. Now it is hard to see how a person who is not willing to rise up on Easter morning can perceive this profound truth. It does not matter who he is, if he is not willing to experience the resurrection, his evaluation cannot do justice to the person of the Master. Things that are spiritual can only be discerned through spiritual eyes.

The preceding treatment has not given any space to a discussion of the form of the resurrection. That question does not arise in the present context. We are simply concerned with the theological significance and implications of it. The next question to be dealt with is the light the resurrection throws on the divine-human relation in the life of Jesus Christ.

LIGHT ON THE DIVINE-HUMAN RELATION: THE RESURRECTION (*Continued*)

The resurrection does not present any psychology of Jesus. It does not even give any material from which a modern psychologist can build a psychological portrait of the inner life of Jesus. The phenomenon of the divine-human relation is such that no psychology has either tools or capacity to comprehend the mystery. We would, therefore, mention the main points made patent by the floodlight of the resurrection.

Firstly, the divine-human relation or the incarnation is a fact from the very birth of Jesus. And, speaking of incarnation formally, it is a persistent and unchanged fact of his whole life. In this context the beginning and the end of his life are identical. He is the incarnation. Secondly, whereas the incarnation as a fact is true, yet the inner meaning, i.e., the revelatory and redemptive content, and progress and growth of his life, are not the same at different stages of his life. He is a growing person, and his moral and spiritual growth is as real as his physical.

Thirdly, the divine and the human in this relationship of growth are neither passive nor inert. They are both active. And this action is interaction. The interaction cannot bear the same ratio because of disparity between divinity and humanity. By disparity I mean that God is existent already and does not start in the embryonic fashion, whereas the human is not existent before and does start in an embryonic way. The human would, therefore, impose certain restrictions on the operation of the divine and thereby, for the time being, create an inequality of interaction.

Fourthly, the resurrection is the very point of perfect identification and unity between the divine and the human movement. It is where God and man are one. It is the point of perfect relation and communion. Standing at the vantage point of the resurrection, one can see the picture of a man moving Godward. Behind him follows the rest of humanity. He was with humanity as one of its members and had his conflicts, temptations, and tensions. He overcame them and became one with his Father and now leads all humanity to be reconciled with him. Summing up all things in himself, he stands subjected to God, to the end that God be all and in all. But *concurrently* with this picture one sees the same man who faced God with humanity, now facing men as their Savior and Lord. There is nothing between him and God. He is very God of very God. The resurrection point reveals this strange unity which logical reason shuns as ridiculous and irrational. But the person of the Christ is the unity of these two dialectically opposed sides.

Fifthly, the unity of the divine and the human in Christ is not a matter of essence. It is relational. As a matter of fact the Christ is the "Relation" that subsists between God and man. It is the Relation in which the two are involved but not as a matter of essence. It is a relation of involution and not of identity.

Lastly, a relation of this type, which cannot be explained altogether by any known categories of interpretation, is unique and stands by itself. It is *sui generis*. Other phenomena in human history may hint at it, may anticipate it; but they cannot create it. On the contrary, given this, they gain their proper value and perspective.

The Nature and Meaning of the "Relation"

Now the stage is reached when the nature and meaning of this " relation " should be dealt with a little more carefully. Let us first see briefly what forms it has assumed in the history of Christological thinking. On the whole, the Christological formulations run the same gamut that is prescribed by the relation of God to the world. There are, however, many characteristics peculiar to the Christological situation that are not considered in a discussion of the relation between God and the world. These will become apparent as our presentation proceeds.

The general pattern of the relation between God and the world is covered by three major considerations, with many slight variations and modifications. The first type of relation is that God is the sole reality and the world is only an appearance. The appearances are mere modes for the manifestation of divine reality. When that purpose has been accomplished the appearances, having served their purpose, are dissolved. This is generally considered the Platonic description of the relation between God and the world. There is, however, another doctrine in Plato that has exerted considerable influence on Christian thought. It is the theory of participation. The world of phenomena does participate in the world of forms. We shall discuss this more when we arrive at our third type of relation.

The effect of such a cosmology on Christology would be that the divine would be regarded as the only real element in the person of Jesus Christ. The humanity would be unreal and insignificant. It would be a means to an end. The center would be divine, and humanity would be on the periphery. The divine would be the sole active power, and the humanity would remain passive. Docetism would be the end result, or humanity might be retained only in some mutilated form. Apollinaris is the classic example of this type of Christology, which has not lost its charm and appears over and over again in the history of dogma. H. M. Relton's *A Study in Christology* is the recent full-fledged defense of such a view. Emil Brunner's *The Mediator* also minimizes the humanity of Jesus Christ. The second type of relation between God and the world can be called deism. After creating the world, God lets it go to work out its own destiny. The world is like a mechanism; once started on its way it needs no more manipulation. The relation is a dualism in which the terms of relation are external to each other. The relation is static and spatial. Applied to the person of Jesus Christ, it results in a theory of parallelism, by which the divine and the human are considered as two separate persons artificially conjoined. Such a view has been traditionally attributed to Nestorius and is known in the history of dogma as the heresy of Nestorianism. Recently Bethune-Baker and Loofs have tried to show that Nestorius could not be accused of that heresy. However, wherever such a view is held, some corollaries also follow. These are the problems of two consciousnesses and two wills. The traditional way of splitting up the sayings of Jesus as divine and human, because in one aspect he spoke as divine and in another aspect he spoke as human, is a direct consequence of such a view.

The third view advocates the dynamic relation between God and the world. The world is a real existence though not absolute. God is not isolated from it at any time. God upholds and sustains the world, but that does not deprive the world of its finite freedom and endless creativity. On this premise the person of Jesus Christ would be the union of God and man in which the two are dynamically related. Such a union does not confuse the terms of relation. The Platonic doctrine of participation and especially its Aristotelian modification in which the separate realm of universals was abandoned helped in the formulation of such a view. Today some Christologies have been formulated under the influence of the philosophy of organism and emergent evolution. The most distinctive of such attempts are Father Thornton's *The Incarnate Lord* and Norman Pittenger's *The Word Incarnate*.

The union of Godhead and manhood in Jesus Christ has been conceived variously. Some reduced the union to mere identity, producing thereby the heresy of Monophysitism and its corol-

lary Monothelitism, which means that there was one will because there was one nature. Others conceiving the union merely
on the ethical level have emphasized the moral quality of the
humanity of Jesus. Jesus in this way becomes the greatest moral
genius among great seers. He is supreme and unique above
all. From Paul of Samosata, Peter the Lombard, Peter Abelard
to the late Canon Hastings Rashdall such a view has been held
and defended in one way or another. Such a view often de-
generates into adoptionism.

There is another view that makes a sort of amalgam of this
union and leads one to believe that the psychology of the God-
Man must be different from the psychology of human beings.
William Temple, in his *Nature, Man and God,* seems to hold
such a view.

There is a distinguished line of theological thinkers who pro-
pose that union between God and man is effected by God's emp-
tying himself of his glory or metaphysical attributes. They are
called kenoticists: Thomasius, Martensen, Charles Gore, P. T.
Forsyth, and H. R. Mackintosh are some of the most prominent
names. Such a view is based on the exegesis of the Christological
passage in Phil., ch. 2. Modern New Testament exegesis has,
however, proved the weakness of such a view being derived
from that passage. Such a mutilated God is hard to conceive.

Ritschl's philosophy of value judgments remains noncommital
on the nature of the union. However, by affirming that Jesus
Christ has the value of God for us, he opens the way for saying
that in Jesus Christ, God and man have met. His metaphysical
bias kept him away from making the point explicit. But a conclusion that the ascription of divinity to Jesus Christ is a subjective projection would be contrary to the intentions of Ritschl.

Schleiermacher tackles the question at the psychological level.
The self-consciousness of Jesus is the locus of his God-consciousness. The God-consciousness is so powerful in him that it determines everything. Humanity is entirely passive, and the possibility of temptation is entirely denied.

It is, however, William Sanday who tries to resolve the Christological puzzle on purely psychological premises. He takes his clue from the psychology of the unconscious. In his *Christologies Ancient and Modern,* he says that the subliminal consciousness is the proper seat or *locus* of the deity of the incarnate Christ. The connection between consciousness and subliminal consciousness is a " bottleneck " relationship. It is horizontal rather than vertical. The difficulty with such a view is that it does not realize the impossibility of determining the *locus* of deity. Moreover recent researches in depth psychology have disclosed that the unconscious is the seat of demonic as well as creative tendencies.

Karl Heim has presented a new Christology under the motif of " leadership." Jesus Christ is the great Leader whose authority is absolutely binding and unquestionable. In this world infected with original sin we need a leader to save us from the polarity of our existence. This is done by Jesus Christ, not by giving a set of rules, but by the " I-Thou " relationship. This relationship which the immediate disciples of the Master had with him in their lifetime is now available to us of the succeeding generations, through the Holy Spirit. In this way Jesus Christ becomes our contemporary. Such a Christology might help people who have suffered at the hands of a bad leadership, but is in no way able to throw light on the depth and profundity of the person of Jesus Christ. W. M. Horton, in his book *Our Eternal Contemporary,* follows the lead of Heim, to whom he also dedicates the book.

D. M. Baillie, in his book *God Was in Christ,* has made a serious attempt to do justice to both the sides of the person of Christ. He takes his clue from the idea of prevenient grace. The goodness of Jesus Christ is every bit a human achievement, but because it is made possible through the grace of God, it is in the first place the goodness of God. God is logically prior. This logical priority of God, I suppose, would mean that the relationship between God and man in Jesus Christ is simultaneous. So far the concept seems to be helpful; but he goes on to say that the divine prevenience is " the conditioning and the determinative "

factor. This will make the divine the center of the person of the
Master and thereby endanger his humanity. This will defeat the
author's purpose of keeping the two sides in the proper perspective. His main difficulty arises from not starting from the unity
of the person of Christ. He converges on him, so to say, from the
side of God and man, but never seems to arrive at and disclose
the point of convergence. The idea of divine prevenience also
stands in danger of rationalizing sin. "Faithful souls in Israel had
long been wrestling with the dreadful things that were allowed
to happen among men; and this came to a head when Jesus was
condemned and crucified. This was the worst thing that had
ever happened through the sin of men. Yet they came to believe
that this was also the best thing that had ever happened in the
providence of God." Could they make a statement like this before the resurrection? Does it imply that sin invariably serves the
ends of good and is, therefore, necessary to good? Or are there
sins and sins? What is the criterion of judgment, etc.? Is it not
true to say that in the Christological situation, although the divine is prior, neither God nor man taken singly are determinative? The determining factor is the "togetherness" of God and
man.

Karl Barth (*Church Dogmatics,* Vol. IV, Part 2, pp. 55–57)
criticizes the Christology of D. M. Baillie. According to Barth
the mistake of Baillie lies in his trying to understand the *unio
hypostatica* in Christ in the light of the *unio mystica* of Christian
experience. "Even Donald Baillie ought to have considered this
before he too — quite innocently of course, and without being
guilty of the flagrant extravagances of Biedermann — made it
his business to try to interpret Christ in the light of the Christian rather than the Christian in the light of Christ."

Barth grounds his own Christology on the exegesis of John
1:14, "The Word became flesh," where the word "became" or
its Greek equivalent *egeneto* is interpreted in the light of *labon*
of Phil. 2:7. "The Word became flesh" means then "The Word
assumed flesh." This is further interpreted in the light of Luke
1:32, 35. It is God himself through whom the man Jesus is born

(*Church Dogmatics,* Vol. I, Part 2, p. 201).

The theological doctrine which Barth develops from this exegesis is called *anhypostasia* and *enhypostasia.* One is negative and the other positive. The negative means Christ's human nature does not exist in and by itself but is only a possibility of divine existence. *Enhypostasia* asserts that " in virtue of the *egeneto,* i.e., in virtue of the *assumptio,* the human nature acquires existence (subsistence) in the existence of God, meaning in the mode of being (*hypostasis,* ' person ') of the Word. The divine mode of being gives its existence in the event of *unio,* and in this way it has a concrete existence of its own, it is *enhypostatos.*" (*Church Dogmatics,* Vol. I, Part 2, p. 163.)

Barth elaborates this doctrine and defends it against the charges of one-sidedness and diminution of humanity in sections 64 and 65 of Vol. IV, Part 2, of his *Church Dogmatics.*

Emil Brunner, in his *Christian Doctrine of Creation and Redemption,* reverses the procedure of his earlier Christological work *The Mediator.* There he started with the Person of Christ and followed the deductive method. Now believing that the Person of Christ can best be discerned through the work, he adopts the inductive approach. Whether this will succeed where the earlier approach proved unsatisfactory remains to be seen. " But the real intellectual problem," says Brunner, " of the doctrine of two natures, that is, how to conceive the union of the two natures in Jesus at the same time, is beyond us. We must certainly hold firmly to both statements without reduction: true God, true Man. Thus, for instance, we must not make the attempt, which many people thought they could discern in my work on *The Mediator,* to deny to Jesus full human personality " (p. 360).

Bultmann got around the quest of the historical Jesus by identifying the meaning of Jesus with his message. The essential point of the message is that it demands a decision for God. Paul Tillich asks the radical question about the power for decision. The power for decision is a gift and not a demand. It comes from the new reality which is the New Being in Jesus as the Christ. This means that " the last avenue of the search for the historical Jesus is barred, and the failure of the attempt to give a foundation to the Christian faith through historical research becomes obvious" (*Systematic Theology*, Vol. II, p. 106). This means the New Being appeared in finite existence in a personal life; but the unique historicity or the name of that personal life cannot be guaranteed. It is not indispensable for faith.

Nels F. S. Ferré in his *Christ and the Christian* has done for American theology what Donald Baillie did for British theology in his *God Was in Christ*. He advances the thesis that the category of Spirit is the key Christological category because it can explain, among other things, the phenomenon of interpenetration in the hypostatic union of God and man in Jesus Christ. He works constructively between the limits of recapitulation and *enhypostasia*. His discussion of these subjects is very refreshing and instructive.

John Knox in a series of delightfully written monographs presents the position that the event Jesus Christ is at once complex and integral. The elements of complexity can be designated as the personality, life, and teachings of Jesus, the response of loyalty he awakened, his death, his resurrection, the coming of the Spirit, the faith with which the Spirit was received, and the creation of the community. No one of these elements can be sacrificed and together they form an indivisible historical moment. Although the various elements cannot be dispensed with, it soon becomes evident that the element of the community plays a major role among the elements and in the thinking of John Knox. One is left with the impression that Christology has been subordinated to ecclesiology.

Oscar Cullmann, in his *The Christology of the New Testament*, develops a phenomenological analysis of the various titles of Christ. The analysis covers the early, pre-existent, present, and future works of Christ. One total picture of the Christ-event arises out of this detailed discussion. The Christ-event is the center of *Heilsgeschichte* which leads from creation through reconciliation in the cross and the invisible present Lordship of Christ to the still unaccomplished consummation in the new creation

(p. 324). According to Cullmann, "all Christology is *Heilsge-schichte*, and all *Heilsgeschichte* is Christology" (p. 326). He develops an *ebed Yahweh* or Son of Man Christology. He prefers the latter because of its adequacy and greater scope. The two ideas of *representation* and God's *self-communication* play a decisive role in construction of this Christology. At the end of his discussion on the Son of Man, Cullmann expresses the hope that some modern theologian would undertake to build a Christology entirely on the New Testament idea of the Son of Man. This is a call for a modern Irenaeus to arise!

Vincent Taylor, in his *Person of Christ*, also discusses the various titles of Christ. He, however, comes to the conclusion that the Christology underlying the New Testament is of a variety of kenoticism. In agreement with Forsyth and Mackintoch he sums up his position by saying that "no just reason has been given why, within the limitations necessary to the incarnation, the attributes of omniscience, omnipotence, and omnipresence should not have remained latent or potential, existent, but no longer at the center of the Son's consciousness and in conscious exercise, but undestroyed and capable of manifestation in appropriate circumstances. This is the contention of Forsyth and Mackintosh and I do not think that it has been effectively challenged" (p. 293).

Dean W. R. Matthews, in *The Problem of Christ in the Twentieth Century*, has reviewed again the idea of a psychological solution of the Christological problem.

It becomes clear from the history of dogma that the famous catechetical schools of Alexandria and Antioch set the pattern for the method of treatment with regard to the person of Jesus Christ. The Alexandrians emphasized the deity of Jesus Christ and thereby imperiled his humanity. The Antiochians, being the founders of the historicocritical method, emphasized the humanity and endangered the Godhead of Jesus Christ. The Lutheran theology follows in the main the Alexandrian tradition, as the Calvinists do the Antiochian. When a union was effected between the Lutheran and Reformed Churches, a mediating school of theology came into existence. Its chief representative was Dorner, who wrote the classic *History of the Doctrine of the Person of Jesus Christ*. He tried to save both divinity and humanity from being underrated, the one at the expense of the other. He emphasized the growth of Jesus' humanity. His construction of Christology is based on an elaborate relation between faith and philosophy. Coming at the time when people cherished distrust of metaphysics and when the advance of natural sciences had confirmed their doubt, it did not grip the hearts of the people. Against this background we can see why Ritschl exercised so much influence.

From the above brief survey the need for preserving the two sides of the person of Jesus Christ becomes urgent, and the necessity of interrelating the two classical approaches quite obvious. The following pages endeavor to reinstate that truth.

What then is the relation and how can we describe it? Firstly, the relation is of mutual involution. It refers to the basic fact that the two are involved in the relation, yet by no means exhausted by it. So also, Godhead is not exhausted in any fashion that would warrant our asking who now rules the universe, etc. God's entering into relationship does impose some limitations on him, but does not imply his being encircled. Yet it is hard to deny that when God enters into relation it is the totality of God in relation in so far as God is God at every given point of his relation. A similar statement from the side of man would also hold true. Jesus Christ is an individual man. In him all the human individuals are not realistically present. He does not exhaust mankind. But at the same time he is not an isolated human being. He is the representative man also. In him and through him the whole of mankind is related to God.

Secondly, the relation implies mutual interaction. Looking from the high point of the resurrection down to the very beginning of the life of Jesus, it is extremely difficult to perceive any interaction. As a matter of fact for a long time the divine side of the relation seems to be more or less potential. This does not mean potential over against actual, because God is actual. But in so far as the relation is concerned God seems to be more or less quiescent.

From the age of discretion and from the baptism to the crucifixion there seems to be a tremendous interaction and interplay. Experiences, such as the temptations, the baptism, the Garden of Gethsemane, and the cross show unmistakably the intensity and profundity of this interaction. Neither humanity nor divinity is passive, both are active and affected by each other. The effect on humanity makes for its deep spiritual and moral growth, and expands it in relation to the rest of mankind. The action on divinity creates a new relationship between God and man. Godhead has come within so close and intimate a relationship to man that the two have become inseparable. The only analogy to it is the relation between God and creation; but this, even though close, is not personal and intimate. A revolution has taken place in the relation between God and man. You cannot separate man from God. The God-Man has significance for eternity. And, because this took place within time and history, it changes the value of time and historical existence.

Thirdly, the relation is of interpenetration. From involution, through interaction, we have come to interpenetration. This is the deepest point of identification between the two. The man Jesus is victorious over the forces of evil, and his manhood is transparent. Every tendency that had the possibility of absolutizing itself was overcome by the profound love and trust in God the Father who was the deepest reailty of his being. The cross is the symbol of conquest over the demonization of finiteness and its freedom. Sin is conquered on the cross; for sin is the act of finite freedom to declare itself as unconditioned. God is so deeply involved in human redemption that he does not turn away from sin, the very opposite of his love; he overreaches sin and reconciles humanity with himself. The two movements, as we have said before, meet at one point of identification — the point, which from one angle refers to man and from another to God. This point of identification is what we call the Christ. The resurrection shows par excellence how Godhead and manhood have personally met together. This happens in the concrete and historical life of Jesus Christ. But what happens is not limited by time and space. It changes time and space and has eternal consequences. History has a different direction, and the destiny of man is changed.

Fourthly, the relation discloses a unitary person. To the questioning mind this does not make sense. How can the two dialectically different form a unity? Of course, if we mean that according to the canons of strict logical necessity the divine and the human form a unity, the questioner would be right and we wrong. But that is not our meaning. The New Testament presents a unitary, integrated person. He is not a psychopath or a split personality. It may be that the New Testament by presenting the Christ in such a way tells us of a unity that is higher than reason can comprehend and which appears to it irrational. In the nonrational and alogical unity of his person the two are related without contradiction. The person is unitary. His witnesses corroborate this fact. And finally, he who appears illogical to reason is not irrational in himself. He does not suffer from a basic contradiction. As a matter of fact, he is the point of higher unity — the unity of the person. The resurrection presents and bears witness to the reality of wholeness. From the resurrection point of view the contradiction is removed and the conflicting parties are reconciled. Resurrection is reconciliation and identification made patent. The Christ is the reconciliation and identification point. In him on the spiritual-ethical level reconciliation has been effected, and this now can be applied to the cosmological sphere, disclosing thereby the oneness and the unity of all existence. But this first and foremost happens in the Christ. The Christ is, therefore, the one who provides coherence, unity, and reconciliation to the world. He is not, by any logical exercise and stretch of imagination, a contradiction in himself. He appears so when reason confronts him; he is so when reason attempts to resolve him into a system. It may be that for apprehending him a different tool is required.[1]

THE RELATION IS SUI GENERIS

It is hoped that the above considerations have borne out the singularity of this " Relation." Such a phenomenon is not present anywhere else. It is nonrepeatable and *sui generis*. What constitutes it as such has already been explained in one form or another; but here we state it again in different terminology. Who is the Christ? The Christ is the meeting place of the eternal, the universal, on the one hand; and of the historical, temporal, and particular, on the other. The eternal by itself would be the ever-present ground of existence, and its relation to the particular modes of being would be general in the sense that the particular modes would not really count. The emphasis is on the common ground shared by all particular manifestations. The historical, on the other hand, would be marked out by its particularity and uniqueness and would stand in complete isolation from other particulars except that the spatial continuum might create an illusion of relatedness. The emphasis of the historical and of the temporal side is on particularity and on individuality. The emphasis is on the difference and on the uniqueness. This would be isolation and divorce from relationship.

The two by the principle of mutual exclusion are half-truths and therefore distortions of truth. The two in relation would constitute the most decisive category. In Jesus Christ the two meet in such a way that the eternal does not simply use the particular and the individual as means to an end, nor does the particular shine in its own solitary splendor. The two are related in such a way that in the higher unity of the person of Christ the two are one without contradiction. This, of course, is not a metaphysical truth first and foremost. It is first religio-moral and then cosmological and metaphysical. Thus Jesus Christ, by being the unity in his person of the Eternal God and of the historical, particular man, is the most decisive category. He is *sui generis*.

It may be urged that the Christ cannot be absolutely decisive, for God through his immanence is related to all particulars, and that between Christ and others there is only a difference of degree rather than quality. It is true that the immanence of God implies relation to all particulars and that by personal realization some individuals will be more closely related to the divine presence than others; so much so that some will be ahead of others. But if this proposition, which seems to us to be true so far, goes on to affirm that the eternal, universal, immanent presence enters into relation with a particular being in such a way that their relation is absolute and not relative, and then goes on to cite a historical instance where this has been reported as having happened, then the assertion of the New Testament writers must be considered redundant. But in the whole history of religion and thought such an event has not been reported from that premise.

The question, however, cannot be decided on the level of mere immanence in its metaphysical significance. Metaphysical immanence is a background concept; but the decisive sphere is the spiritual-ethical, and the kind of immanence of God at this level differs from the first. The metaphysical immanence is a neutral existence, but God's presence relevant to the spiritual-ethical sphere is meaningful. The spiritual and religious history of mankind shows the reaching down of God toward man and the reaching out of man toward God. This is through and through a qualitative movement. It is in this qualitative movement that Jesus Christ appears as the God-Man — the decisive point where God and man finally met to stay together. Such an event bears a twofold relation to the spiritual and religious history of man. In the first place it is the fulfillment of the spiritual quest of man — his longing to meet God. It is fulfillment because God has reached down to answer man's quest.

In the second place Jesus Christ is the judgment. He destroys all distortions which have taken place and which might take place in the spiritual history of man. In the qualitative movement he appears as its criterion. The relation of the criterion to the qualitative movement is one of finality. In this respect Jesus Christ is the center of history. His coming is the *kairos* — the time of fulfillment and the fulfillment of time.

The spiritual history of man is reflected in the distinct histories of nations. Jesus Christ appears within history in the Hebraic prophetic tradition, because it of all traditions was most capable of receiving him. He is within history, although he discloses the meaning of history. The Christ, however, cannot be deduced from the immanence of God, though one may anticipate such a happening on that basis. Neither from the Greek nor from the Hebrew point of view can the Christ be deduced and arrived at. He is expected in both in one form or another. As a matter of fact the immanence of God gains its true evaluation from the fact of the Christ. Immanence shows the possibility of meeting between God and man. The Christ shows the actuality and thereby enables the possibility to gain concretion. Apart from the Christ the true meaning of God's immanence remains hidden. When God and man have met in the way they have in Jesus Christ, then and then alone immanence can be adequately evaluated.

From this relation of the Christ to God's immanence we can gain much light on the allied questions of analogy and approximation to truth. Logical thinkers and systematizers have built a ladder of systems to God on the basis of analogy. Nearly all the classical proofs of the existence of God are based on analogy in one form or another. But, being true in part, they invariably fail to bring God to us or us to God. The partial truth that analogy contains is that it hints at or anticipates the truth. As such, analogy remains ambiguous and would never satisfy the religious quest. But the important fact to note is that it does not arrive at God. Analogy itself gains proper proportions if God and man have really met. How can we understand that which is analogous to God, unless God is presented to us? As we have shown before, the rabbis were unable to arrive at the Christ. By no stretch of imagination, Old Testament scholarship maintains, could the Jews relate together the Suffering Servant of God and the exalted Son of Man. Similarly no Hellenist in his right senses would allow the Ideal to suffer from the permanent marks of scandal by flirting with particularity. Such a thing would never enter his head. And yet John dares to make the statement "And the Logos became flesh." Yes, it is true that both the Jew and the Greek groped after the Christ and expected the Christ; but they could not present the Christ. Anticipation is always appreciated and evaluated on the basis of fulfillment, and analogy, on the basis of the truth. The Christ is the fulfillment and the truth. So also people before and after Jesus, speaking historically, have expected the Christ. Their tireless religious pilgrimage after God and their appropriations of God's nearness cannot be treated lightly. They contain a profound truth. But apart from the Christ they remain isolated shafts of light — glimpses of reality. The Christ is their fulfillment. The fact of Jesus Christ discloses the unity and universality of the quest for truth. He also discloses its meaning and the point of focus and fulfillment.

Furthermore, a word is necessary by way of explanation of the Christian experience itself. The experience of the Christian shows approximation to the stature of the fullness of the Son of Man. This adventure continues in the direction of quality even in the life to come. By becoming the sons of God we never displace Jesus Christ. He is the basis on which we become the sons of God. He is the one who gives us the power and the light to be the sons of the Heavenly Father. He is primary; he is the cornerstone; he is *sui generis*.

CONTEMPORARY HINDU THOUGHT

To know oneself is to know all we can know and all we need to know. (*Eastern Religions and Western Thought,* by S. Radhakrishnan, p. 61.)

He, verily, who knows that supreme Brahma, becomes very Brahma. (*The Thirteen Principal Upanishads,* translated by R. E. Hume, p. 377.)

THE PHILOSOPHY OF RADHAKRISHNAN

HINDU IDEALISTIC THOUGHT has always found receptive ground in America. Emerson, Whitman, Thoreau, and many others gave it wide currency through their literary works. The New England transcendentalists and others who were out of sympathy with the organized churches turned to it for fresh life and light. Ever since Swami Vivekananda appeared on the platform of the Congress of World Religions in Chicago, this type of Hindu thought has become more and more popular among certain circles.

Then something drastic happened in the academic circles of philosophy that paradoxically increased its appeal. Neo-Hegelianism, which was the reigning philosophy in British and American centers of learning at the turn of the century, suddenly began to disappear under the attacks of logical positivism, naturalism, linguistic and logical analysis. Neo-Hegelianism had had a popular appeal as well as an academic standing. When it was replaced by a different and highly technical philosophy a vacuum was created because the current thought had no relevance for the common man's religious and moral experience. This vacuum has been exploited by the multiplication of esoteric half-religious and half-philosophic sects and movements. And if one looks deep into them, the underlying substratum is advaitic or nondualistic Hindu monism.

The best way to describe this change of fronts in the philosophic and religious situation is to use the word "metaphysics." Current philosophy abhors the word "metaphysics" and all that it stands for, whereas these sects proudly call themselves metaphysical. There is an exact antithesis in attitude. Even existentialism is afraid to use the word "metaphysics" because of the academic prejudice against it. It substitutes the word "ontology" and means by that the structural analysis of man. These sects alternate between the philosophic and popularly religious aspects of metaphysical philosophy.

The two outstanding contemporary religious philosophers of India who have found hospitable response in America are Radhakrishnan and Aurobindo Ghose. Both are modern thinkers and endeavor to relate the ancient idealistic thought of India to the scientific Western world views. However, Radhakrishnan has lived and taught in the West and has mastered the art of communication of ideas. He is widely known and read. His inclusion in the Library of Living Philosophers is both a recognition of his stature as a philosopher and as a representative of the grand tradition of idealism — a lineal descendant of Śankara.

A study of the philosophy of Radhakrishnan in its own right and in relation to Christological thought will be very helpful in understanding the phenomenon of religious syncretism and the situation of the churches in America.

A. C. Underwood probably spoke prematurely when he said regarding Radhakrishnan, "He is a historian of philosophy rather than a creative thinker." [1] This judgment would have to be modified, especially in the light of Radhakrishnan's *An Idealist View of Life*. This book sets forth his scheme of ideas in a systematic way. One would desire that he pursue farther some of the implications of what he has said; but one must confess that in this book he has presented his system of ideas with many creative and profound insights. " Taken as a whole the system is, indeed, an admirably ingenious attempt to reconcile the claims of the two opposed and apparently irreconcilable concepts of change and eternity." [2]

With this brief introduction we shall first discuss his general scheme of ideas, then the new elements and modifications that he has introduced into the general pattern of Hindu thought, and finally we shall add a few words of criticism. In the next chapter some special problems of his philosophy will be discussed in relation to our view of the Christ, and the relevance of this discussion in the context of this book will become apparent.

The following is not an exposition of the total philosophy of Radhakrishnan, a task too big for the present undertaking, but only a selective approach. It is hoped that no misrepresentation is made of the distinguished Indian thinker.

THEOGONIC AND COSMIC PROCESS

The basis of all that is, is the Absolute. The Absolute is complete, nothing can be added to it and nothing can be subtracted from it. The Absolute is incapable of increase.[3] The Absolute is whole, which means that no differentiations exist in it. It is pure unity, which does not mean that it is a mere abstraction. The Absolute is not only complete in itself but is also all-inclusive. Nothing can or does happen beyond or without it. Nothing, however, affects the Absolute. It is beyond any touch or taste, however viewed. The Absolute is ananda.[4]

Then, without much explanation, Radhakrishnan posits of the Absolute necessary growth. " It is the nature of the Absolute to grow into the world." [5] Here is introduced a principle of differentiation, and the wholeness of the Absolute is broken up. This is the beginning of the theogonic as well as the cosmic process. The distinction of self and not-self arises. The first existent and his opposite are born. The first existent is God, Iswara, and his opposite is maya, prakriti or the not-self. " The first existent or object in the Absolute is God, Iswara, or the world soul. He is the first-born Lord of the universe, the creator of the world and its ruler. The Absolute breaks up its wholeness and develops the reality of self and not-self. The self is God, and not-self the matter of the universe." [6]

An important distinction should be made at this stage. The Absolute is the realm of infinite possibilities. The theogonic and the cosmic process is, therefore, the actualization of only one possibility. Why this one particular possibility is chosen out of the infinite possibilities, Radhakrishnan professes he does not know.[7] This process shows two things with respect to the Absolute. In the first place, the Absolute *qua* Absolute is the pre-cosmic or pretheogonic Being. And in the second place, the actualization of one possibility does not by any means exhaust the Absolute. The Absolute, therefore, is known, if at all, on the basis of this one possibility. It is known as God from the standpoint of this actualized possibility, but viewed aside from this it is the Absolute. It is not quite clear whether God is a real being or simply a manifestation of the Absolute or its symbolic representation. Although we will examine the relation between the Absolute and God more precisely later, here for the sake of continuity of thought, we simply register the remark that Radhakrishnan regards God more as a symbol than a real being.

THE WORLD

The original duality of self and not-self is differentiated further, and thus the manifold universe of our acquaintance arises. It is not explained how this further differentiation takes place. Most likely it is due to the necessity of growth out of which the first duality arose. " By the further differentiation of this original duality of self and not-self, Iswara and Maya, the whole universe arises." [8] The cosmic process is neither self nor not-self. Both of these are necessary and organically related.[9] The separation of the two would lead to the dissolution of the cosmic process. The two are indeed indispensable. Yet another relationship obtains between the two — the self or God is logically prior, not temporarily anterior, to the world and is called its creator and ruler.[10] God is creator and ruler in the sense that he stands in an organic relationship to the world. He is the principle of creative advance and regulation of the maya, prakriti principle. He is thus involved in the cosmic process. The process has meaning for him and fills a deep need in him.[11] The cosmic process, on the other hand, has no effect on the Absolute.[12] The Absolute is its ground and the world process is dependent upon it.

God and the world are not identical until the very end. At every stage of cosmic development there remains " an unrealized residuum in God." [13] At the end of the cosmic process God and the world become identical. Two basic conceptions are involved here. First, if it is affirmed that God and the world are identical as such, then the world would be lost to us as appearance and sheer illusion. To Radhakrishnan the world is neither illusion nor an independent existence but a relative existence. Second, by saying that God and the world are not identical, he has introduced the principle of growth; and still more, this growth is not merely the evolution of that which is involved but an emergent evolution.

Unlike the philosophers of evolution, Radhakrishnan conceives of an end to the process. The end is the spiritualized harmony of all that is.[14] At this stage God and the world become identical, and the world process comes to an end. And finally, God or the cosmic process relapses into the Absolute; and that is the end and the fulfillment of all things. The circular movement is complete. The Absolute, the ananda, is the beginning and the end.

THE PERSONAL GOD

The above discussion has not taken into consideration another level of thought in Radhakrishnan. There is no hard-and-fast distinction between the two levels. They are ingeniously related. However, for the sake of clarification and adequacy of treatment we shall now present his scheme of ideas on a religio-moral-psychological level. The first part of the discussion may be regarded as philosophic over against what follows.

The background for this level of thought remains the same

identical, differenceless, impassive, complete, and all-inclusive Absolute. The appearance of first duality of self and not-self Iswara and maya also forms part of the background. In place of the philosophic concept of the many or what is called "further differentiation," there is at this level the religio-mythological idea of the Fall. Just as the further differentiation of the original duality implies the existence of multiplicity on the basis of growth and individuation, so also at this level the Fall implies the breakdown of the immediate and unitive character of life. "The Fall symbolized the disintegration of the harmony, the lapse from the primeval condition into division, from a unitive life into a self-centered one." [15] The result of the Fall is individualization, separation, and isolation. Man has become individualistic and self-centered. He has obscured his basic identity with the Brahman-Atman principle. He has caged the infinite in the tight and narrow prison of the flesh. This suppression of the Atman is philosophically due to the principle of maya, but subjectively or psychologically it is due to avidya. Man through avidya puts more premium on the local, particular, and partial values. He clings to false ideals and values and thereby forsakes his essential being which is the Brahman. His existence becomes fragmentary and his outlook devoid of the vision of the whole.

The pure consciousness of Brahma when united with avidya becomes man. Man, therefore, has a dual existence. One is his ideal self and the other his empirical self. His ideal or essential self is identical with Brahma. Nay, it is *Brahma: Tat tvam asi!* It is the spectator-self; it is not touched by the pain and anguish, joy and ecstasy, growth and decay of the empirical self. The intelligible self is the proper subject of metaphysics, and the empirical self forms the subject matter of psychology. It is the empirical self that tastes and smells, loves and hates, feels and is cold, grows in strength and falls a prey to sickness and disease. It is a teleological unity and is concrete, busy, and dynamic. "What we call a person at any stage is the cross section of the growing entity." [16] The empirical self is an organized whole, but it is distinct from the real self. This organized empirical self, being infected with avidya, regards itself as absolute and completely independent. Individualism is its great sin, for it regards multiplicity as ultimate. To regard multiplicity as final is to fall under the spell of maya. Our distinct existences are only temporary. Maya lends them the semblance of eternity. Under its influence we endeavor to preserve the hard outlines of our separate existence, forgetting that individuality is merely one of the conditions of our existence in space time.[17]

From the preceding discussion it becomes obvious that the break-through of the empirical self to the ultimate substratum would be true *moksa,* or salvation. It is the aim of religion and the achievement of it constitutes the ethical process. But before saying anything about the ethical process a word or two should be said about the law of karma and rebirth. The law of karma is an assumption, and Radhakrishnan only undertakes to interpret it in his own way. The individual is not able to rid himself of avidya in the span of one life. He therefore needs more than one life, and this means rebirth. The law that causes these births and rebirths is called karma. It is because of the karma (actions) that the individual has done that he is born again. His past never leaves him until he has achieved unity with Brahman. Karma, according to Radhakrishnan, is the principle of connection with the past, and has a determining effect. But it is not wholly deterministic. It bears room for freedom, whereby an individual has a chance to improve his lot. Radhakrishnan makes his point clear by using the game of cards as an illustration. "The cards in the game of life are given to us. We do not select them. They are traced to our past karma, but we can call as we please, lead what suit we will, and as we play we gain or lose. And there is freedom." [18] Karma, then, is a principle of necessity and freedom. Radhakrishnan does not lay much stress on its being a retributive law. It is more a principle of continuity,[19] and is in no way opposed to creative freedom.[20]

Regarding rebirth he says: "The individual has appeared and disappeared times without number in the long past and will continue to be dissolved and reformed through unimaginable centuries to come. The bodily life is an episode in the larger career of the individual soul which precedes birth and proceeds after death." [21]

The soul is not left disembodied when it leaves one body and transmigrates into another. It is invested with a subtle body called *sukshume* or *linga sarira*. As a matter of fact this seems to be the subtle garb of the soul all the time during empirical existence, and it attracts the physical elements to form a physical vehicle on its pattern. The major question of Hindu thought is how to get rid of this rebirth. This brings us back to the ethical process. The ethical process is largely based on the Yoga system of Indian philosophy. The system of Radhakrishnan, and for that matter most of Indian philosophical thought, is based on the foundation of the Vedanta and Yoga. [22]

The Yoga system in itself does not require a god. The following ethical process is based on the yoga. The man goes through three stages of purification. These stages are not by any means clear and distinct as they appear. In a process they are integrally related, although a certain distinction can be maintained. The task consists in breaking through the crust of individuality and reaching deep down into the depth of the soul and realizing our identity with our essential self. We cast off the alien elements. It is, to use Plato's terminology, an act of recollection. The self is always there; we simply have to recognize it. We shall give the different steps of the process in Radhakrishnan's own words. As the basis of the process " it is assumed that the real nature of man, his inherent capacity for the divine, cannot be obliterated." [23]

" The process starts with a quiet introspection, the tiny beginning of spiritual contemplation. By a repetition of a text, or by focusing the mind on an external object such as an image, we try to banish intruding thoughts and collect ourselves. *Dharana* is concentration. It is the control of will, of attention. To chain the mind, which is generally compared to a restless monkey, to a single object is not easy. Irrelevant thoughts will drift in, desires and worries will disturb, and with an effort can we fix our mind on the chosen subject. When attention becomes less discursive and concentration deepens and mind ceases to wander we get into the state of dhyana, or meditation. The soul becomes empty of every thought except the one meditated on, which takes possession of it. When it is awake only to the reality to which it is directed and all else is forgotten, *ekagrata,* or one-pointedness, arises. Out of the brooding darkness, illumination is won.

" While outer knowledge can easily be acquired, inner truth demands an absolute concentration of the mind on its subject. So in the third stage of samadhi, or identification, the conscious division and separation of the self from the divine being, the object from the subject, which is the normal condition of unregenerate humanity, is broken down. The individual surrenders to the object and is absorbed by it. He becomes what he beholds. The distinction between object and subject disappears. Tasting nothing, comprehending nothing in particular, holding itself in emptiness, the soul finds itself as having all." [24]

It seems quite clear now that individualism is to be abolished and an effort is to be made to achieve an " impersonal universalism." This, however, does not imply that when some individuals have achieved this state then the world process comes to an end. These perfected beings retain their individuality and help others achieve their salvation.[25] This is Radhakrishnan's conception of social salvation. When all are saved — and that surely will be the case sooner or later if the love of God is at all real — then the world process will come to an end.

Following the lead of Deussen, Radhakrishnan brings out the ethical meaning and the social conception of salvation in another way. He interprets the formula " *Tat tvam asi* " (" That art thou") as lending itself to active social service. That text according to Deussen is " in three words the combined sum of metaphysics and morals." The Gospels, says Deussen, truly proclaim, " Love thy neighbor as thyself "; but they do not explain or say why. By the constitution of nature I feel pain and pleasure in myself and not in my neighbor. The answer then lies in " *Tat tvam asi.*" I love my neighbor as myself because I am my own neighbor or my neighbor is myself. Radhakrishnan says: " Every person round me is myself at a different point of space and time and at a different grade of being. When one realizes that beings are but the self (*atmaivabhut*), one acts not selfishly but for all beings." [26]

God, in what we have described as the second level of thought, is conceived in a much more personal fashion. He is in the world and engaged in the process of salvation of the world. God acts in a threefold way: as Brahma, he creates; as Vishnu, he preserves and redeems; and as Siva, he judges. " These three stages represent the plan, the process, and the perfection. The source from which all things come, the spring by which they are sustained, and the good in which they enter are one. God loves, creates, and rules us. Creation, redemption, and judgment are different names for the fact of God." [27] God is more than the cosmic process at the different stages of growth, but at the end God and the cosmic process are identical.

The fact, however, still remains that the personal God, or Iswara, stands under the shadow of maya and cannot be identified with the Absolute. God and the world recede into the Absolute. The individuality is lost and the world fulfills itself by self-destruction.

Our justification for pointing to two levels of thought in Radhakrishnan lies in the fact that on one level the emphasis is on the Absolute and on the other the stress is laid on the personal God. It is nevertheless true that the over-all emphasis is laid by him on the Absolute.

SOME MODIFICATIONS OF INDIAN PHILOSOPHY

Radhakrishnan as an interpreter and expositor of Indian philosophy considers it as a unity. To the casual observer it appears as a jumble of conflicting notions. But in the manifest variety there is a deep underlying unity. According to him, this substratum of unity is furnished by the Vedanta philosophy. He also conceives of Indian philosophy as a growing entity. He believes in retaining the general framework of ideas provided by the seers of ancient India, but it has to be widened, modified and made up to date by constructively relating it to the advance of contemporary scientific knowledge.[28] He himself is one of those who have made a heroic effort in relating the wisdom of the ancient East to the scientific knowledge of the modern West. He has, therefore, been instrumental in the modification of Indian thought, both in eliminating certain elements from and in adding certain elements to it. He is one of the most important and powerful forces behind the movement called "the New Hinduism."

Radhakrishnan has introduced a new notion into the body of Indian thought. It is the notion of emergent evolution. God or the world soul is the basis of it. Throughout the process of growth and evolution there always remains a residuum to be realized. This makes for the appearance of novelty and creative advance. The process of evolution is not simply the making actual of that which is always potential. It is more than that. It includes an element of newness and creativity. It is a characteristically Western notion, but the general scheme of Indian thought based on the Vedanta does lend itself to a notion of evolutionary growth. Whereas, as we observed earlier, the Western formulation of the process is not directed toward an end or comes to an end, in Radhakrishnan it definitely comes to a climax and an end.

The law of karma receives an interesting treatment in the hands of Radhakrishnan. In popular thought the law is considered to be the stern administrator of retributive justice. It is to the popular mind the only explanation of the inequalities in life and the suffering thereof. The mechanical working of the law of karma has engendered a philosophy of pessimism and fatalism. An attitude of resignation is the only alternative in the face of stern, predetermined fate.

Radhakrishnan abandons the popular conception and seriously modifies the retributive aspect of the law. His interpretation is much more philosophic. The law of karma is a link with the past, but that does not imply that an individual's present is entirely determined by his past. The law of karma implies a broad conditioning of the present by the past, but there is enough scope for the individual to mend his ways and secure for himself a better future. The law has, therefore, a twofold significance: first, it is the law of necessity which means that past and present are related in the form of continuity; secondly, it implies freedom of action and a hopeful shaping of the future. The karmic law is then the law of freedom and necessity.

Although there is no way of telling whether the law of karma is prior or posterior to rebirth, yet as a matter of practical consideration rebirth is governed by the karmic law. Here again there is a wide divergence between Radhakrishnan and popular Hindu thought. In popular Hindu thought the quality, morphology, and opportunities of each next birth are determined by the kind of life led in the previous one. Though man can be reborn as a man, or even as a man of better quality and status as in the three higher castes, he also is in danger of being born as a fowl, a fish, or a beast, in strict accordance with his karma.

Radhakrishnan rejects this popular notion and interprets the fish, fowl, and beast as merely symbolic. The popular thought means to convey that the person born has those qualities, but is not actually fish, fowl, or beast. A man is reborn as a man, however ignorant or imperfect. Radhakrishnan retains the doctrine of rebirth because the chances of a lifetime are too meager to accomplish the salvation of an individual. He needs more opportunities and a longer time. Since every life in the long run will be saved, if the love of God is a reality, it follows that it takes much longer than one brief span of life to accomplish the redemption of a man. The same would be true of mankind as a whole.

This leads us to make a few remarks about the social conception of salvation in Radhakrishnan. This is not quite peculiar to him. From Raja Ram Mohan Roy to Mahatma Gandhi, Indian leaders have emphasized it. However, it does gain a peculiar force when interpreted by Radhakrishnan. The end of the cosmic process will not be reached until every last individual has been redeemed. This means that the perfected individuals, such as Jesus and Buddha, do not lay aside their individuality. They keep it and help others to achieve that state of impersonal universalism where individuality will be discarded. That the perfected souls do not pass on but wait and help the weaker brethren is what constitutes social salvation in the thought of Radhakrishnan. It is a powerful way of affirming the common destiny and inherent solidarity of the human race. When humanity as a whole has achieved impersonality, individuality is abolished. It all becomes " *Tat tvam asi* " (" That art thou ").

Some Critical Remarks

We shall now try to offer a few words of criticism. The criticisms will be brief because the brief sketch of Radhakrishnan's philosophy offered above does not permit us to indulge exhaustively in criticism.

Although the specific relation between the Absolute and God is a special subject for discussion for the next section, yet it is not out of place to say that Radhakrishnan's discussion of the subject is very puzzling and confusing. God is nothing but a symbol. He is not a real being. It is certainly confusing from the religious standpoint to call God personal, for he is not a real being at all. The concept of God is adopted on the basis of usefulness and convenience. It is an accommodation to the weakness of men's minds. The stalwart in spirit do not need him.

There is a further confusion of God and maya. He calls God logically prior to maya and the creator and ruler of maya, or prakriti. But Iswara, or the personal God, is under the shadow of maya and is not the Absolute but less than the Absolute. This seems to imply that a certain relationship between the Absolute and maya produced God, or Iswara. In that case maya would be logically prior to God and would be in part his creator.

The doctrine of evil or sin is interpreted largely in the sense of error. The objective aspect of error is maya, and the subjective is avidya. The error is based on man's finitude. Man's mistake lies in his confusion of things transitory and temporal with things eternal. The Real is always there, but it is obscured by man's preoccupation with finite ideals and values. This attitude of man is largely one of error, and the moment the Real is recognized the error disappears. The finite is essentially the infinite. We have just to look beneath the surface. This conception of evil as error does not take into account the seriousness of the fact of moral evil. It fails to interpret evil in its religio-moral actuality. It only interprets evil in the sense of tragic guilt, which simply means that error befalls man because of his finitude.

Radhakrishnan does not discuss freedom in any profound sense. Freedom is one aspect of the law of karma, and it implies that, although man's present and future are determined by his past, they are not so absolutely. There is then within necessity an element that provides the individual with a chance to make the best of his present opportunities and thereby improve his future chances. This is the broad way in which Radhakrishnan discusses freedom. He fails to raise the question of the tragic nature of freedom. He does so because the general pattern of his monistic philosophy cannot permit the question. The tragic nature of freedom consists in the stark reality that the free individual can so use his freedom as to deny his own being and face extinction. This brings us to another point, that is, universal salvation.

By making the love of God the final determining factor Radhakrishnan asserts that, this love of God being real, no individual can be lost. Here again emerges the point we made above, that he does not attribute real freedom to man — freedom that would entail the possibility on the part of man of denying and defying the love of God. Since this element is lacking in Radhakrishnan he without much justification assumes that the fact of the love of God will itself redeem the individual and all individuals. It is clear that the appeal of the ideal is exaggerated and the possibility of man's rejection of it underestimated.

According to Radhakrishnan, the uniqueness of man is temporary and coterminous with the cosmic process,[29] although sometimes his language seems to imply more. At the end of the cosmic process the individuality of man is lost. He sinks into the undifferentiated Absolute. But, arguing against the conditional immortality idea of Pringle-Pattison, he accuses him of not recognizing the " ineffaceable " worth of human personality. If Radhakrishnan means that the ineffaceable worth of man is an abstract value ultimately preserved somewhere, then it is simply an abstract value and the question of man or individual is irrelevant. If he means that the ineffaceable worth is temporary, then it is a misuse of language. It must then be stated that Pringle-Pattison's doctrine does more justice to the worth and freedom of the human individual than Radhakrishnan's.

As we have noted before, Radhakrishnan modifies the Hindu doctrine of rebirth. The following points have to be kept in mind while criticizing this doctrine. First, if our universe is an actualization of one possibility out of the infinite possibilities belonging to the Absolute, we can then discuss rebirth only in this context; rebirth in other possibilities would mean idle speculation. Second, in the scale of evolution man is a very recent appearance, and compared with the life of the universe his life is the merest fraction. To say that " the individual has appeared and disappeared times without number in the long past " must either mean that ever since the appearance of man in the universe the human individuals have appeared and disappeared — if so, the past is not by any means long: it is very recent — or, it means that the individual *qua* individual and not necessarily as man has appeared in countless forms and disappeared to appear in more in the future. Then what we call man was once born in all the different forms of possible existence as evidenced in the evolutionary scale. And now having become man, he does not revert back to a primitive form. But this has nothing to do with karma; it is due to the logic of the evolutionary process. On the basis of karma there is no reason why a man who behaved like a beast should not return to the status of a beast; but it is the horizontal evolutionary movement that lays down the law against relapse. The karma has nothing to do with it. Radha-

krishnan confuses karma with evolution. Third, karma and rebirth are a vicious circle, for without karma there is no rebirth
and without birth there is no karma. In order to get out of this
vicious circle karma is raised to the status of a law by the process of abstraction, and a distinction arises between karma as law
and karma as action. This law is later hypostatized and raised to
the level of a power. Either it becomes an independent power
or the power of someone. Since ultimately it is not independent
but only the Absolute, it must belong to the unfathomable depth
of the Absolute. In the last resort karma remains a dogma without justification.[30]

Fourth, the relation between karma and rebirth is necessary.
For only those are born who have acted. If once the karma-
rebirth nexus is fixed, there does not seem to be any room for any
real break-through or the emergence of novelty. The number of
individuals thus born may be unbounded, but once the nexus is
established the limit is set. This contradicts the creative power
of the divine Being, for the limitation is external.

Radhakrishnan's language is extremely ambiguous. He freely
uses terminology that in Christian thought connotes something
else, to justify to men the ways of the Vedanta. Although at the
time of reading it is very lucid and pleasant, yet when all factors
have been taken into consideration the result is ambiguity. There
is an underlying confusion or vacillation running through the
system of Radhakrishnan. The Eastern framework has not quite
achieved a creative synthesis with the content of Western science. This point will be further elucidated in the next chapter.

GOD, THE ABSOLUTE AND THE CHRIST

Wisdom is one thing: to understand the intelligence by which all things are steered through all things; it is willing and it is unwilling to be called by the name Zeus. — Heraclitus. (*Selections from Early Greek Philosophy*, edited by M. C. Nahm, p. 90.)

The great problem of the philosophy of religion has been the reconciliation of the character of the Absolute as in a sense eternally complete with the character of God as a self-determining principle manifested in a temporal development which includes nature and man. (*An Idealist View of Life*, by S. Radhakrishnan, p. 343.)

GOD AND THE ABSOLUTE

IN THIS CHAPTER, as stated before, an effort will be made to discuss some special problems of Radhakrishnan's philosophy. These problems are in a way arbitrarily chosen. They are certainly the crucial problems of his philosophy, and for that matter, of all idealistic philosophy. The fact that they stand in a special relation of relevance to the Christian view of life as inspired by the fact of Jesus Christ has determined the selection of these problems. These problems are the relation between God and the Absolute, Atman and the jivatma, and Brahman and the world. After we have discussed these problems, we shall proceed to examine the relation of these problems to our view of Jesus Christ.

The whole discussion of God and the Absolute and their interrelation is based on the analysis of human nature and its needs. This analysis looks at human nature from a twofold point of view. It depicts man as a divided and dichotomous being. The dichotomy consists, on the one hand, of man's emotional and devotional needs, and on the other, of the intellectual and mystical demands of his nature. In response to these two distinct sides of human nature there are two corresponding divine sources of fulfillment. There is, however, a third element that transcends this dichotomy and harmonizes the two sides of man's nature. This element is called " religious " or " intuitional," and presents man as integral and whole. Therefore, correspondingly, the divine does not appear now as God and then as Absolute in accordance with man's disparate nature, but as one Being. The ultimate Reality is apprehended as a whole by the religious and intuitional approach of the whole man. The former is man's actual state, and the latter what he ought to be and therefore the goal of the cosmic process.

Lest it should appear that God and the Absolute are mere names and no reality, or that they are nothing but the projections of human needs and demands, we ought to know briefly Radhakrishnan's view of the nature of the structure of existence and possible experience. Naturalism cannot account for everything in the world, particularly the order and the creativity of the world process. The world process requires a creative power to explain it. It matters little how far back we go in space time, because we can never get around it; we are within the space-time structure; we cannot account for it. Thus the rationality of the world process suggests that the creative power which can explain it can be only mind or spirit.[1] " There is an affinity between the structure of the world and the mind of man. Our sense perceptions, our logical concepts, our intuitive apprehensions are not forms superinduced on reality, but are determinate forms of reality itself." [2] The above statements concede the following truth. " No element of our experience is illusory though every element of it has a degree of reality according to the extent to which it succeeds in expressing the nature of the real." [3]

GOD

In accordance with man's emotional and devotional nature
the fact of a personal God is posited. The idea of God is indeed
nothing but an interpretation of religious experience.[4] Man has
some fundamental experiences, and these experiences are understood and explained on the assumption of a personal God. God
is the creator, sustainer, and judge of this world. More especially
he is the savior and redeemer. He is organically related to the
world and is as much dependent upon the world as the world is
dependent upon him.[5] He is, however, logically prior to the
world.[6] Growth, the historical and temporal processes, have
meaning for him and fill a deep need in him.[7] God is love, and
is engaged in the process of salvation; but he cannot save alone.
He needs the help and co-operation of man. In imparting his nature to us he has made us sharers in his creative power. He needs
our co-operation and wants us to respond to his call. This does
not mean that the world would tumble off into ruin if we withhold our co-operation. It simply means that the goal set before
the world will remain unrealized if we fail him.[8] When every individual is redeemed, then the world process comes to an end
and God recedes into the Absolute. But at the different stages
of the world process God and the cosmic process are not identical. He is a creative genius, and it is due to him that there is
novelty and emergence in the world. There is an " unrealized
residuum " in God. " The process of the world is not a mere un-
folding of what is contained in the beginning. It is not a question
of mere preformation. The end of the world is not contained in
the beginning, such that God might retire from the process altogether." [9] God is how the Absolute looks when viewed from
the human angle. Since at the end of the cosmic process God
and the universe become identical it follows that " the universe
is the Absolute dynamically viewed." [10]

We have so far tried to look at God from the human and
world angle, but there is another way of appraising him, and
that is from the side of the Absolute. The Absolute is the realm

of infinite possibilities, and one of these possibilities is being realized in the actuality of our universe. God is the possibility behind this actuality.[11] God is related to the Absolute as its possibility and to the world as a possibility to its own actuality. That is, the relation is logical and not temporal.

THE ABSOLUTE

Just as the religio-moral needs of man demand a God who would take a personal interest in him, so there are other needs of man that require an absolute being. " There are aspects in religious experience, such as the sense of rest and fulfillment, of eternity and completeness, which required the conception of a being whose nature is not exhausted by the cosmic process, which possesses an all-fullness of reality which our world only faintly shadows. This side of religious experience demands the conception of the supreme as self-existence, infinity, freedom, absolute light, and absolute beatitude." [12]

The Absolute is self-existent and the ground of its own being. " All the sources of its being are found within itself." [13] The Absolute is joy, and that means that it is self-existent and self-sufficient.[14] The Absolute is pure, perfect, passionless, pure consciousness and pure freedom. It is all-inclusive, and the question of immanence and transcendence does not really arise for it. It is not an abstraction but infinite possibility. " The possibilities or the ideal forms are the mind of the Absolute or the thoughts of the Absolute." [15] One of these possibilities is being actualized in the form of our universe. Because it is a possibility of the Absolute that is being realized, the Absolute is its ground. But creation does not in any way affect the Absolute. " The Absolute is incapable of increase." [16] Looked at from the standpoint of this specific possibility which is in the process of actualization, the Absolute is its precosmic nature. " As to why there is realization of the possibility, we can only say," observes Radhakrishnan, " that it is much too difficult for us in the pit to know what is happening behind the screens. It is maya, or a mystery which we have to accept reverently." [17] Because the Absolute is self-sufficient it is not necessary for it to express any of its possibilities. Since, however, one possibility has been chosen and expressed it can be attributed only to the freedom of the Absolute. " If this possibility is expressed, it is a free act of the Absolute." [18] Following Gaudapada and Śankara, Radhakrishnan uses the analogy of an artist who creates without effort. It is an overflow from the abundance of the Absolute. " Hindu writers are inclined to look upon the act of creation more as the work of an artist than that of an artisan. It is *lila* or free play." [19] But, as C. E. M. Joad has clearly pointed out, the analogy is not taken seriously. For the artist uses a medium. " He cannot express himself in *vacuo;* he requires paint and canvas, stone and sound." [20] This argues for the reality of the world, a point that we will have to take up a little later. Let us now discuss the relation between God and the Absolute.

THE RELATION BETWEEN GOD AND THE ABSOLUTE

Put succinctly, in Radhakrishnan's words, the relation is as follows: " We call the supreme the Absolute, when we view it apart from the cosmos, God in relation to the cosmos. The Absolute is the precosmic nature of God, and God is the Absolute from the cosmic point of view." [21] Radhakrishnan suggests that the creeds of religion are like the hypotheses of science. On the hypothesis of the electron the physicist tries to explain the physical phenomena and feels that he has given an exact representation. But it is becoming increasingly manifest " that it is simply impossible to form any picture at all of the ultimate nature of the physical world. The theories are symbolic and are accepted because they work." [22] God, then, is a symbol, a real symbol of ultimate reality. Those who feel that the gods of the polytheists, and not their own God, are only symbols are mistaken, in the opinion of Radhakrishnan. " The monotheists are quite certain that the gods of the polytheists are symbolic if not mythological presentations of the true God, but they are loath to admit that their own God is at bottom a symbol." [23] According to him, as we have said before, " God is a symbol in which religion cognizes the Absolute." [24] Although Radhakrishnan conveys a strong impression that God is a real, distinct being, yet the real characterization of God is a symbol. Sentences, such as "God is not the great silent sea of infinity in which the individuals lose themselves, but the divine person who inspires the process first, last, and without ceasing. . . . He is creating now and for all time," [25] are difficult to understand against that background. His language certainly portrays a real being, and we wonder about the meaning of his intentions and thoughts. But to say that God is a symbol does not imply that he is a figment of our minds. [26] "God is a real symbol of the Absolute reality . . . a phenomenon well founded in reality." [27] These statements are in agreement with Radhakrishnan's view of the spiritual unity of the universe. However, he does not say anywhere that the Absolute also is a symbol. He seems to concede this point when he says that the supreme when viewed apart from the cosmos is called Absolute. The Absolute like God is the symbolic expression through which man understands Supreme Reality in relation to those needs which are not satisfied by the symbol of God. It is, however, the main tendency of Radhakrishnan to identify the Absolute with ultimate reality and regard God as the symbolic expression of it.

It is time for us to return to Radhakrishnan's view of the spiritual unity of the world and develop this argument a little further on that basis. God and the Absolute provide answers to the two sides of human nature. Since spiritual reality is consubstantial with the deepest self of men and the universe as a whole is unity of spirit, our "logical concept" and "intuitive apprehensions" are not fictitious but determinate forms of reality. It follows that the symbols of God and the Absolute are determinative of supreme reality. They correspond to the discord and dichotomy in us. Our perceptions of this disharmony are also determinative forms of reality. From all this follows the conclusion that dualism is true and not a fabrication of human fancy. And even if so, it still would have an element of truth. In another context he says: "Even if God be an idea and has no reality apart from one's ideation, that which frames the idea of God and strives to realize it is itself divine." [28] It may be argued that what we feel to be pain, evil, error, disharmony, or whatever one may call it, is nothing but illusion. Although such a statement would be a defiance of hard facts of experience, yet if we accept it to be true, we are not in any way argued out of the situation. It may be that the terms of the dichotomy, pain and evil, are not real, or they are explained away on the basis of the law of karma and rebirth, but the fact that I still think and believe that I suffer, etc., is not illusory. My error is as real as God or the Absolute. Radhakrishnan says: " The principles of karma and rebirth suggest to us that the value of the world is not in any way affected by the actuality of evil, error, and ugliness." [29] Prof. C. E. M. Joad has evaluted the situation rightly: " There is no doubt that I believe myself to suffer and think men do me evil. If I am mistaken in so thinking owing to the illusoriness of pain and evil, my mistake itself cannot be illusory. Thus if pain and evil are illusions, error is not. It is real in just the same sense as God or the Absolute is real." [30] Keeping the hard facts of pain and evil, Joad puts his finger on a major defect of Radhakrishnan's system of thought. " The failure to provide," says he, " an adequate treatment of these undoubted facts of experience is indeed, in my opinion, a definite weakness in Radhakrishnan's philosophy." [31]

In the beginning of this chapter we suggested a third element by which man as an integral being experiences the Supreme Reality in its wholeness. " Philosophers may quarrel about the Absolute and God, and contend that God, the holy one, is worshiped, is different from the Absolute which is the reality demonstrated by reason. But the religious consciousness has felt that the two are one." [32] Let us see in brief what relation obtains between the Absolute and God on the basis of this premise. Although there are only two terms of relation, there are two subterms. These terms in the logical order are as follows: the Absolute, a preferred possibility among limitless possibilities, God and the cosmic process. At the end of the cosmic process,

God and the cosmic process become identical. This means that the specific possibility of the Absolute has been actualized. The possibility, God, and the cosmic process now are all identical. Thus the real relationship is not so much between God and the Absolute as two distinct terms but of the Absolute to its own actualized possibility, which really implies that there is no relation whatsoever, for there is no " other." Thus Radhakrishnan concludes: " On this view there cannot be any ' creation.' The question as to why the Absolute limited itself, why God became man, why the perfect became imperfect, is irrelevant. For there is no such thing as infinite which first was an infinite and then transformed itself into the finite. The infinite is the finite. The Absolute is the self and its other." [33] We cannot, however, stop here. We must raise some questions that Radhakrishnan does not raise, and therefore does not answer. What is the relation between one possibility and another in the Absolute, and between the limitless possibilities and the Absolute itself? Since one of these possibilities is being actualized and after actualization will return into the Absolute, it is obvious that it would no more remain a mere possibility and the relation that it bore to the Absolute, and to its infinite possibilities could not be the same after actualization as before. Would anything happen to the Absolute in the light of this new element? If not, then the relation would be nothing but a parallelism and no point of identity would exist. This will lead to an unmitigated dualism! Again, what relation do the different elements of a realized possibility bear to it?

This last question helps us to bring out another side of Radhakrishnan's thought. From the preceding considerations on the nature of the Absolute we would be led to believe that he has been true to his professed belief that if the game of philosophy is played squarely without any interference from religion, the end result would be absolute idealism.[34] However, this absolute idealism does not seem to be what goes by the name of pantheism, implying thereby the identity between the Absolute and the world. Radhakrishnan believes in the relative existence of the world, and even interprets Śankara in the same way.[35] " The indwelling of God in the universe does not mean the identity of God with the universe." [36] Therefore what he posits is a " positive idealism " or " dynamic monism." He concedes that pluralism is true and valid " within limits." Therefore: " What we want is a dynamic monism capable of accounting for a growing universe with its time and change." [37] Thus Radhakrishnan seeks a middle path between abstract monism and radical pluralism while rejecting these two extremes. " Abstract monism, which destroys personal values and reduces individuality to illusion as much as radical pluralism, which means chaos, and relies on good luck and harmony of the world, is a defective attitude of life." [38] We can conveniently sum up this aspect of his thought in the following words of his: " The Absolute is not an abstract unit, but a concrete whole binding together the differences which are subordinate to it. The whole has existence through the parts, and the parts are intelligible only through the whole. The values we find and enjoy while on the way to it are preserved and receive their full supplementation in it. They are not annihilated." [39]

We shall withhold criticism until the relation of Atman to jivatma or the ideal self to the empirical self has been discussed. The previous discussion of God and the Absolute renders unnecessary any independent examination of Brahman and the world, for we have really dealt with the problem although we have not mentioned the word " Brahman." It is the Sanskrit equivalent for the English " Absolute " in Vedantic philosophy.

ATMAN AND JIVATMA

The governing notion behind the Self as subject and the self as object is quite prevalent in the upanishadic literature. In the *Mundaka Upanishad* the idea is figuratively expressed as follows:

> " Two birds, fast bound companions,
> Clasp close the selfsame tree.
> Of these two, the one eats sweet fruit;
> The other looks on without eating." [40]

In interpretation Radhakrishnan says: " The former is the empirical self and the latter the transcendental self." [41] The empirical self is the subject matter for psychology and the transcendental for metaphysics. Radhakrishnan conceives of the primordial state of man as a harmony with nature. Innocence and immediacy prevailed and there was no division and separateness. But then there comes a break, which is attributed to man's rationality and self-consciousness. " The break in the normal and natural order of things in human life is directly traceable to man's intellectuality, the way in which he knows himself and distinguishes himself from others." [42] Radhakrishnan describes this break of man from nature and harmonious living in three stages. In the first place man begins to think and imagine a dark and uncertain future full of fears and hopes. The very thought of it inspires similar uncertain and mixed feelings. In the midst of it he is struck by a fundamental insecurity; death seems to be inevitable. The knowledge of death instills in him a deep fear that sets him in desperate search for escapes and solutions. He feels himself opposed to the cosmic process; and nature, which gave him birth, appears to him as his enemy. This creates in him a feeling of frustration. Secondly, his essential innocence, unity with nature and fellow feeling having been impaired, he begins to look at human beings as his enemies. He becomes selfish, acquisitive, and defensive. He looks upon himself as " lonely, final, and absolute." Thirdly, the above two factors divide him hopelessly inside, and he falls a prey to fragmentariness. " His identity splits, his nucleus collapses, his naïveté perishes. He is no more a free soul." [43] This is largely the story of man's empirical self. The empirical self is a system of logical and psychological energies.[44] It is a growing, dynamic thing and " what we call a person at any stage is the cross section of the growing entity." [45]

This organized whole called the personality or individuality is quite distinct from the transcendental self. The latter is the " persistent substratum," the " unseen seer," and remains always distinct and unaffected by the fortunes or misfortunes of the former. " The subject of experience is said to be distinct from every moment of the experience. It is the persistent substratum which makes all knowledge, recognition, and retention possible." [46] Clearly expressed, the relation between the Atman and the jivatma is as follows: " Inconceivable though it is, the Atman has nothing to do with the individual's life history, which it so faithfully attends and accompanies. Assumed as the constant witness the Atman serves merely as a screen or the basis on which mental facts play." [47] The Atman, or the intelligible self, is universal and all-pervasive and cannot be demonstrated.[48] It is the universal basis on which common experience of a common world is possible.[49] We can distinguish four terms in this relation. The first two are the Atman as universal self and as related to an individual. This is only a logical distinction. It is the same self-identical self. The other two terms are the empirical self and the not-self. These two form a unity.[50] Thus there emerge two major terms of relation; but there is no real relation, for when the universal self, which in its relation to an individual is obscured and hidden, becomes manifest then the seeming duality disappears and it is the selfsame Atman. And this Atman is the Brahman.[51] The individuality of man is only an interim affair. It is necessary during the cosmic process, and when the process comes to an end individuality is lost. During the cosmic process individuality is conceived in two ways. In the first place, it is looked upon as self-love which hides and obscures the divine in man. Secondly, it is a center of action and is necessary as long as the cosmic process lasts.

The above interpretation of Radhakrishnan's thought betrays a definite inclination toward abstract monism. There are, however, passages that argue for a concrete monism. " The phenomenal character of empirical self and the world answering to it is denoted by the word ' maya ' which signifies the fragility of the universe. Maya does not mean that the empirical world with the selves in it is an illusion, for the whole effort of the cosmos is directed to and sustained by the one supreme self, which though distinct from everything is implicated in everything." [52] It is the nature of this implication that we want to know and investigate. Radhakrishnan is not at all clear on the point.

Let us carry the discussion a point farther before we embark on the criticism of some of Radhakrishnan's ideas. This point is based on his conception of social salvation. There are individuals who have attained salvation, which means that they have transcended their historical individuality. Since a large number of people still need to be saved, Radhakrishnan says that these liberated souls retain their individuality as centers of action whereby they can help others. It is indeed arbitrary to say that the liberated souls retain their individuality once they have gone beyond it. It must mean that eternity is implicated in history in a positive manner, but Radhakrishnan does not make the point clear. He does not go far enough.

In the interrelations of God and the Absolute, Atman and jivatma, and the saved and the unsaved, we detect a definite hesitation, an indecision that makes him waver between monism and dynamic idealism. We see that we are confirmed in this criticism by Prof. E. L. Hinman's view that a "vacillation" runs through the thought of Radhakrishnan. "While he is speaking of the surrender to be made to the spirit of the whole, he is a Hindu and a Vedantist, a pantheist if you please." "So soon, however, as he yields himself to the logic of concrete idealism, he stresses development, growth, gradual progress toward perfection." [53] This confusion in Radhakrishnan is because of the interim nature of the cosmic process. At the end of the cosmic span all comes to an end. The real question consists in asking about the nature and meaning of the relative existence of the world; and in the second place, whether what is achieved here is or is not annihilated in the Absolute. The second part of the question would be answered if we had a satisfactory answer to the first. Here again we have the same hesitation, which is very typical of him. The following quotations will make our meaning clear. "We rise from life to thought and return from thought to life in a progressive enrichment which is the attainment of ever higher levels of reality." [54] "It is the function of religion to reaffirm the intuitive loyalty to life and solidarity of human nature, to lift us out of the illusion of isolation and take us back to reality." [55] The first passage shows the enriched and highly differentiated harmony, whereas the second, though it may be interpreted otherwise, makes us return to the instinctive and undifferentiated harmony of life and nature.

How does Radhakrishnan bring out the relative existence of the world? He does it by showing that God and the world are not identical in the stages of growth. There is then during the period of growth and advance a distinct existence of the world. But the transcendence of God is only an internal transcendence, and this is eliminated when the two become identical. God is the world in the end, and there is no distinction left. The possibility has been actualized and therefore the distinction that previously obtained between possibility and its progressive actualization has diminished to zero. It is clear that this kind of relative existence of the world is not real; it is somewhere between the relative and illusory existence. It would have been a real relative existence if in spite of the realization of the possibility God still retained transcendence in virtue of which he could never be exhausted by the world. In asking what relation the actualized possibility bears to the Absolute we have asked the same question in different words. This argues that if some determinate aspects of the Real are involved and grounded in the actual and so also by reciprocal implication the features of the actual are preserved in the Real, a further characterization of ultimate Reality becomes necessary. Thus pluralism is not only true " within limits," i.e., within the cosmic process, but is implicated in ultimate Reality. This does not indeed make pluralism the final truth, but it does make it an essential element in the picture of Reality as a whole. Similarly, ultimate Reality as a unity is involved in pluralism and by no means exhausted by it. In this context individuality as laying claim to absolutism would be denied. But, in so far as it aligns itself with the pattern of ultimate Reality, it is affirmed and preserved.

But Radhakrishnan does not believe in the retention of individuality beyond the cosmic process. In his book *The Reign of Religion in Contemporary Philosophy*, he adheres to positive monism and promises to develop it in a systematic way sometime in the future.[56] This promise has been fulfilled in his *An Idealist View of Life*, unless he is intending to write a much more elaborate work. " These lectures," he says, " state my views on some of the ultimate problems of philosophy." [57] If the later book is to be considered as truly representative of his thought, then it is hard to see how he has fulfilled the promise of a systematic exposition of concrete idealism. In the earlier book he very significantly concluded by saying: " The Absolute, therefore, is the whole, the only individual and the sum of all perfection." " The differences are reconciled in it, and not obliterated." " The values we find and enjoy while on the way to it are preserved and receive their full supplementation in it. They are not annihilated." [58] Although abstract monism is represented by many passages, we quote the most typical. " When we see Brahman we become Brahman." [59] However, according to the expressed intention of Radhakrishnan, we take the former quotation as representative of his philosophy. We feel that in his Hibbert Lectures he has not kept to the line of his declared intention. He says, " The central question is whether the self loses or retains its individuality." [60] The answer, of course, is that the individuality is lost. " The loss of individuality happens only when the world is redeemed, when the multiple values figured out in it are achieved. The world fulfills itself by self-destruction." [61] At the end of the cosmic process God who is identical with the cosmic process recedes into the Absolute. Thus everything is absorbed into it. When individuality is lost a state of impersonal universalism prevails. Prof. C. E. M. Joad calls it " an ultimate submergence of all life in the static perfection of the Absolute." [62] Thus it would appear that a later expression of his philosophic convictions has carried him away from concrete idealism to abstract monism. Whether this has been accomplished in the spirit of true speculation or by the seductions of " the reign of religion " is hard to decide. For Radhakrishnan hastens to add, " This view is not pantheistic, for the cosmic process is not a complete manifestation of the Absolute." [63] Let us clearly envisage the difference between the two positions. In his earlier book he gave us the understanding that differences are not eliminated in the Absolute. They are reconciled. In the second book the differences are obliterated. Other things being equal, this is an extremely important difference and does not show a development in the direction of concrete idealism. The submergence of all things in the Absolute, from the standpoint of this universe, makes Radhakrishnan a pantheist. For the identity of the world is lost in the Absolute and has become the Absolute in so far as the relation of the Absolute to all its possibilities must be uniform. However, from the side of the Absolute, since the Absolute has other possibilities in addition or in exclusion to this specific one, Radhakrishnan cannot be called a pantheist. This one possibility does not exhaust the Absolute. But if in the never-ending creative activity of the Absolute the same fate is to be dealt out to other possibilities as will befall this one possibility, and there is no indication to the contrary, then it is only a matter of time: ultimately it would be pantheism.

There is, however, another way open, and in this the arguments of both books uphold him. He can be called a positive idealist with reference to the cosmic process only so long as God and the cosmic process do not become identical. Positive idealism in this sense would be only provisional and pragmatic but not a characterization of ultimate Reality. It is true because it works and not because it is so intrinsically. There may yet be another avenue open. It may be argued that the Absolute is inexhaustible, not only in the order of time but by its very nature and constitution. In that case the question that we have raised before would be raised again: What is the relation that subsists between the Absolute in that capacity and its actualized possibilities? This certainly would be of the nature of reciprocal implication. But Radhakrishnan has not forged any tools to cope with this difficulty. He is, however, conscious of the problem. " The Hindu is aware of this fundamental problem and as early

as the period of the Upanishads we find attempts to reconcile
the doctrine of the changeless perfection of the Absolute with
the conviction that God is also responsible for this changing
world."

THE RELATION OF CHRIST TO RADHAKRISHNAN'S PHILOSOPHY

"Christianity," says Radhakrishnan, "represents a blend of the
Hebrew and the Greek traditions, though it has not yet suc-
ceeded in reconciling them." [64] It is our conviction, however, that
if this problem finds solution anywhere, it is and will be within
the scope of Christian thought. We shall now proceed to relate
Radhakrishnan's interpretation to our view of the Christ.

Our starting point will be individuality, and if we succeed in
showing that the Christian view does not abolish individuality,
our discussion of the personal nature of the divine will become
considerably easier. As we observed earlier, Radhakrishnan uses
individuality as a source of evil, and secondly as a temporary
base of action whereby it works against itself. Before we go on
any farther it is important to note that for him there is no distinction between personality and individuality. Personality at any
time is a cross section of a growing entity. It is organic. He
uses the word "individuality," in the main, to cover personality
also. In Christian thought, however, there is an important distinction between individuality, as representing the image of nature in man, and personality, as representing the image of God
in man. These two are not by any means separate or to be separated or in any relation of juxtaposition, but are very delicately
related. Man is spirit-body unity.

In Radhakrishnan, since the goal is "impersonal universalism,"
to be Brahman or Atman, individuation, individuality, and individualism, as representing one general trend, are all false-
hoods, and if they are true at all, it is only in the pragmatic
sense. He does not see individuality in any other way except
as a distortion and therefore to be dispensed with as soon as
possible. "When all individual spirits are perfected, God himself will relapse into the Absolute, creation being thus at once

ransomed and annulled by the cessation of the impulse to in-
dividuate." [65] Man's finiteness, his individuality, is a prison
house for the universal ever-present Atman. The prison has to
be destroyed or swallowed up in order to perceive the real
self in its reality. The moment the individualistic distortion of
the universal and all-pervasive self is destroyed, the individual
is also eliminated.

This, however, is not the case in the Christian scheme of
things. In our view of the Christ there arises a third conception
of individuality, which is not covered by Radhakrishnan's two.
In Jesus Christ individuality or finiteness is also destroyed.
Finiteness embodying and affirming man's desire to be infinite
or absolute is overcome. The theme of the temptations is the
effort on the part of evil forces to persuade Jesus Christ to
affirm himself in his historical individuality as the supreme.
The whole life of Jesus Christ, and particularly the cross, bears
witness to the phenomenon of the destruction of individuality
as laying claim to absolutism. On the other hand, by positive
righteousness he made himself so transparent to the divine
that no contradiction remained between divinity and humanity. The relation of perfect union was achieved. By making
humanity transparent, by stripping it off from any possibility
of its asserting itself in its own right, the humanity was not
by any means absorbed in the divinity but only became completely responsive. Therefore the God-Man not only is a reality
in history but is also beyond it.

It may, however, be argued that individuality is a category
of possible existence and is not applicable, except by contradiction, beyond it. But if it is conceded that eternity and
time stand in a relation of reciprocal implication, the essential
truth contained in individuality cannot be given up. On this
premise the human individual as a partial creator and enjoyer
of values can never be destroyed. This thought is present in
Radhakrishnan's earlier volume, but its implications are not
at all worked out. He says: "The Maya theory simply says
that we are under an illusion if we think that the world of in-

dividuals, the pluralistic universe of the intellect, is the absolute reality. Pluralism is true only within limits. But it has to be transcended, that is, completed and supplemented, and not rejected and abolished." [66]

In the concept of social salvation emerges the basis of a better estimate of individuality, but again Radhakrishnan does not develop it. If the liberated soul, after having transcended the two conceptions of individuality, still retains it and does not relapse into the karma – rebirth nexus, then there must be another conception of individuality that is not opposed to divinity. On the other hand, individuality thus defined can be a means for the manifestation of divinity. He seems to return to this idea in the introductory essay to his edition of the *Bhagavadgita.* We shall examine this line of thought more closely at the end of this chapter. This brings him once more close to positive idealism; but we shall see how far he has really improved his position.

The transition from this point to the next can be made by a quotation from the *Philosophical Review,* where Professor Hinman says, " Professor Radhakrishnan seems to have a Hindu's distaste for theism and personalism, which he can hardly bring himself to interpret in other terms than those of limitation." [67] This view would be confirmed by what we have said about Radhakrishnan's conception of individuality. During the cosmic process human individuals limit the actions of God. God in order to save the world has to overcome the resistance of individual wills. Also the world environment limits him. So when the world is saved and the individuals are perfected, there is no resistance and no limitation to God. Since God was personal only in relation to this limitation of the individuals and environment, and this limitation has been abolished, God cannot any more be conceived as personal. " If God has no environment on which he acts, he cannot be personal." [68]

In the Christian scheme inspired by Jesus Christ the situation looks somewhat like this: First, limitation cannot always be conceived as an external relation; it can be internal also. In calling God personal, the limitation that is implied is self-limitation, something peculiar to the being and nature of God. It simply means that God's being is internally defined and not something diffused and chaotic. It signifies that God knows himself as himself. Secondly, the saved world, by the logic of reciprocal implication, stands in a new relationship to God; but this is not of limitation in the sense used above. The saved universe is transparent to the presence of God. He penetrates it through and through. This pervasive presence of God does not, however, eliminate distinctions. Individuals are not lost; they have become transparent but remain distinct. There are no differences, but there certainly are distinctions. Radhakrishnan himself says that pluralism is not rejected or abolished but supplemented and completed.

Thus God does not cease to be personal, for our relationship to him is never abolished. It is, no doubt, altered. This relationship, however, does not imply that just as God can penetrate us so can we penetrate the immeasurable depth of his being. We can never exhaust him. He is inexhaustible. It may be well to keep in mind that our use of the word " God " differs from Radhakrishnan's in not making God and the world identical. In our view, God and the world never became identical. God remains transcendent and inexhaustible in virtue of the unfathomable depth of his being. This is quite consistent with his being immanent in the world.

What we have discussed above is no doubt based on our conception of Jesus Christ. Nevertheless, the discussion has been indirect. Now we shall examine the problem of Radhakrishnan's thought in direct relation to Jesus Christ. Although it is obvious, yet it is not out of place to point out that the name " Jesus Christ " in itself represents the unity of two realms. " The Christ " to start with was a title, but it soon became a proper name. The name became symbolic of the reality that the disciples and the Evangelists had experienced in close fellowship with the Master.

The conception of resurrection in Christian thought does not stand for the resurrection of the soul but of the body. The soul, gaining the ground to continue, is not left discarnate. It is clothed with a garment. The idea behind the resurrection is that soul-body is the complete or whole man. The soul is not by itself the whole reality of man. Since the Christian conception of the resurrection is based and derived from the resurrection of Jesus Christ, let us see what the resurrection of Jesus Christ signifies. In his case the resurrection is also the resurrection of the body. The body in general, representing historical individuality, is not discarded. During his stay in history, historical individuality played an important part. The resurrection does not mean the continuance of the selfsame individuality; that could be maintained only at the expense of grave contradiction. The meaning of the resurrection is, however, that he was not disembodied. He had a form suited to his being and the spiritual environment. The form is called " spiritual," " glorified," or "God-given." Whatever the name, the truth is that historical reality is not a shadow or phantom but is taken up into the consummation of things and is preserved in the essential structure of Reality.

In Jesus Christ we have the meeting of God and man. He is the divine-human center. He is the God-Man. He is the relation that subsists between the divine and the human realms. His humanity although always in relation to his divinity is yet characteristically a creation of and in history. It stands for the humanity of an individual and also representatively for every human individual. In principle it represents all historical existence. If his humanity were discarded or absorbed, it would mean that history and the creative and emergent elements in history had no meaning — that history was meaningless and a grand illusion. Christian thought has on the contrary maintained that the God-Man is an eternal fact. By that Christian thought shows how seriously it regards history and historical existence in general. Jesus Christ as the unity of God and man represents that the picture of ultimate Reality is not only divine but divine-human. Temporal and historical existence has made a difference. This is not to argue that this picture exhausts the depths of the divine Being, but that is how ultimate Reality would appear to us. The God-Man is the representation of ultimate Reality as it concerns us and as we are related to it. The only exception is made in the case of those who are able to divest themselves of the essential structures of their humanity. For the rest of us, who are not capable of stripping ourselves from our essential being, the God-Man is the norm of ultimate Reality. In him the criterion appears.

Since the fact of Jesus Christ comes to be within history through the medium of a particular tradition, the Hindu may be prejudiced against it. In spite of this prejudice it should be affirmed that such a happening could only take place within a tradition that was historically, culturally, spiritually, and morally ready. That this was not the state of the Hindu philosophicoreligious tradition need not be disputed.

We agree with Radhakrishnan when he says: "The Vedic thinkers adopted a realistic view of the world. In the Upanishads we have an insistence on the relative reality of the world." [69] Even this statement discloses that in the upanishadic period the realism of the Vedas was already attenuated. But Vedic realism and the upanishadic insistence on the relative reality was lost as an insight over long stretches of Indian history. Radhakrishnan himself confesses: "Unfortunately, the theory of Karma became confused with fatality in India when man himself grew feeble and was disinclined to do his best. It was made into an excuse for inertia and timidity and was turned into a message of despair and not of hope." [70]

The Vedic, like the Greek, tradition did not develop adequate concepts of personality, time, history, and freedom. It is only in recent times that such views have been given some kind of expression in Indian life. They are more explicit in the political struggles of the country. It would not be too wide of the mark to suggest that in the present and the days to come Jesus Christ will be more enthusiastically welcomed. However, where there are great opportunities there are great risks and dangers also.

The Hindu is and would be averse to the reception of Jesus Christ through media which are uncongenial to him. An approach should be made that sees the truth of his tradition and is willing to appropriate it and at the same time carry him beyond it. Maybe the early church fathers can give us a lead in this matter. In order to show that truth in other traditions was not fiction but part of the essential truth, the church fathers put forth the Christian doctrine of the Logos as the pedagogue. The Logos doctrine bears witness to the truth of the reciprocal implication of God and the world. It represents the source of this world. There is no revelation general or special so-called. All truth is integral. In this qualitative structure of truth Jesus Christ is the criterion. He is the judgment and the fulfillment.

Clement of Alexandria says, " The same God that furnished both the Covenants was the giver of Greek philosophy to the Greeks, by which the Almighty is glorified among the Greeks." [71]

A person writing about the Indian thought situation could very well substitute or add the words " Hindu philosophy " and " the Hindus." The philosophic and religious situation of mankind is an anticipation and a preparation for the coming of the Incarnate Word. The relation between other religions and thought traditions is explained by Clement in the following comments on the seventeenth verse of the first chapter of John's Gospel: " Now the law is ancient grace given through Moses by the Word. Wherefore also the Scripture says, ' The Law was given through Moses,' not by Moses, but by the Word, and through Moses his servant. Wherefore it was only temporary; but eternal grace and truth were by Jesus Christ. Mark the expressions of Scripture: of the law only is it said ' was given '; but truth being the grace of the Father, is the eternal work of the Word; and it is not said to be *given,* but *to be* by Jesus, without whom nothing was." [72]

This needs to be written up in modern terminology, but the essential truth is there. This way might prove more congenial to the Hindu mind, but we must be prepared against the " Gnostic " reaction. This Gnostic reaction has been offered by Radhakrishnan in his proposal of " sharing " and his denunciation of what he conceives to be the exclusive claim of Christianity. The point of his proposal is to show that the Christian claim to uniqueness is essentially intolerant and born of arrogance. In contrast, the Hindu attitude is tolerant and humble. The argument is based on what the so-called Christian nations have done in the past and not on the true genius of Christianity. Furthermore, the proposal is initially biased in favor of a monism of agreement over against a pluralism of genuine differences.

It may be wise for us to examine critically the implications of the proposal of sharing. It is of vital significance and may throw light on the problem of Christian adaptation. Radhakrishnan, by this proposal and by some sharp reactions of Christians to it, seems to have gained some advantages.

First, he has shown that Hinduism is more humble and catholic in spirit and that Christianity is sectarian and proud. Secondly, the ranks of the Christians have been more sharply divided. Some say that there is between Hinduism and Christianity more than a mere point of contact, whereas the others emphatically deny any point of contact whatsoever. The result is that the Christian church in India and elsewhere has not been able to develop adequate forms of adaptation, and in the meantime Neo-Hinduism has strengthened and consolidated its position to a considerable degree. The Neo-Hinduists confidently say that they have outlived the Christian onslaught.

What then is this invitation to " sharing " to which the Christians on the whole have not shown much " courtesy "? There are different kinds of sharing, and we shall indicate why Christians are able to accept some and reject the others.

1. *Strategic Sharing.* This intends a common stand of religious forces against the secular movements and tendencies of our age. I cannot conceive of any sensible Christian declining an invitation of this type.

2. *Sharing in the Absolute.* This means that we acquiesce in Christ's being made an Idea or a member of the Hindu pantheon. We are told that individual identity is quite compatible

with religious hierarchism. Radhakrishnan knows very well that this is an invitation to death. The method of Hinduism is absorption. Its missionary method is not so much one of going out as inviting in and thereby squeezing out the lifeblood. It is impossible for Christianity to accept such an invitation. As a matter of history it is only Christianity and Islam that have refused to accept this invitation and have not fallen prey to its seduction. That is why they have survived; all others are in the abyss of the Absolute.

3. *Sharing as a Positive Relationship.* Christianity is not afraid of seeking a positive relationship with Hinduism. It is the genius of Christianity that it brought about a creative and positive relationship between Hebraic and Greek thought in the West. It can, and wants to, do the same in India. The Christians took the initiative in this matter and are still serious about it. This positive relationship keeps the points of agreement and difference in their proper perspective. Sharing does not mean only emphasizing the similarities, it also means a realistic grappling with the points of difference. Radhakrishnan should not chide us for taking thought for our life and not plunging headlong into the abysmal depths of the Absolute. Hinduism gives unlimited freedom of thought, but that freedom is like a prison cell without a roof. You are bounded on all sides although you can soar to the skies. Thought is free, but action is strictly determined by rules and regulations.

Radhakrishnan accuses us of being exclusive. If our exclusiveness is born of power, authority or social superiority or any merit of our own, it should be censured. In fairness one should say that the imperialistic connection of Christianity did lend it that arrogance. But that is not the basis of its exclusiveness. The basis is the conviction that there is in Christianity something that is quite unique. The category of uniqueness is tied up with the conception of history, especially where history is taken seriously. Uniqueness, singularity, etc., are appreciated in the context of a historical religion. Hinduism believes in general rules, principles, and truths. It has very little sense of history. It has, therefore, little or no conception of the category of uniqueness. This is not, however, to deny that Hinduism does not make some claims to exclusiveness. Through its exponents like Radhakrishnan it is pronounced as the ideal religion of the future. It is so versatile that all other religions can have a place in it. Just as the claim of Christianity to a unique revelation is turned into a vice of exclusivism, so also the claim of Hinduism to universalism becomes its exclusiveness. We will let others judge the relative merits of these claims.

But the universalism which Radhakrishnan claims for Hinduism is nowhere expounded as a dogma of that " religion." There were conversions from Saivism to Vaishnavism and vice versa, and different kinds of proselytization went on for centuries on end. The various sects and schools of thought considered their beliefs and practices to be true and according to Scripture and did all that was possible to destroy other systems or convert them to their viewpoint. The synthesizing tendency is of recent origin. It can be traced to the victory of idealistic philosophy over other systems of thought. When Sankara's Advaita was enthroned as the philosophy of India, a possibility arose whereby other systems of thought might become its loyal subjects. The syncretistic movement also gained ground under threat from outside. Islamic, Christian, and other forces from abroad hit so hard at the citadel of Hinduism that in order to survive it had to forge new tools of warfare. It learned much from Christianity and other Western institutions and looked within itself to find a common basis to stand up against enemies from outside. In the histories of nations that is the best synthesizing force. Only the idealistic strand of thought could provide some form of synthetic unity, and Sankara's Advaita was the most dominant type. For the sociocultural side the caste system also helped much.

But syncretism as a conscious movement started in the early nineteenth century with Raja Ram Mohan Roy and the Brahmo

Samāj. It was carried forward by Rama Krishna Parmahamsa and particularly Swami Vivekananda, and still persists in a vigorous form in contemporary Neo-Hinduism. The Theosophical movement and the Arya Samāj also helped. Mahatma Gandhi was a syncretist, and so is Radhakrishnan. As an expositor of Indian philosophy, he reduces all the different systems of Hindu thought to absolute monism. The agnosticism of the Buddha, the realism of the Jainas, and the atomism of *nyaya-vaishesika,* etc., are only different points of the road leading to Advaita. Here in this grand sweep even syncretism seems to have got the better of itself. The situation resembles the struggle of the early church. However, Radhakrishnan himself seems to hint at a conception similar to the Logos doctrine, but does not develop it.[73]

Such an approach if followed consistently would have the advantage of removing the false stumbling blocks of human traditions and their arrogance, but would not lose the real stumbling block — the *Scandalon*. We have seen, however, that Radhakrishnan does not develop the implications of dynamic idealism. Rather, there is a suppression of elements leading toward speculative theism. But if the implications of dynamic idealism are followed through, then he would be forced to abandon his major Hindu presuppositions. Professor Hinman is, thereby, led to question, " Is it possible that the 'reign of religion' in the vicinity of Mysore [74] subconsciously induces a thinker to warp his thought unduly away from the Christian and toward the Vedantic speculation? " [75]

In the introductory essay to his volume on the *Bhagavadgita,*[76] Radhakrishnan raises some similar problems that deserve further treatment. My intention is to deal, not with the entire essay, but with only those problems which have a special bearing on the relation between God and man.

He asks, " How can we identify a historical individual with the Supreme God? " His answer takes three lines of approach: (1) Śankara's Advaita, (2) theism, and (3) his own. We shall illustrate by quotations and comments.

1. " When any finite individual develops spiritual qualities
   and shows large insight and charity, he sits in judgment
   on the world and starts a spiritual social upheaval and
   we say that God is born for the protection of the good,
   the destruction of the evil, and the establishment of the
   kingdom of righteousness. As an individual, Kṛṣṇa is one
   of millions of forms through which the Universal Spirit
   manifests Itself. . . . The *avatāra* is the demonstration
   of man's spiritual resources and latent divinity. It is not
   so much the contraction of divine majesty into the limits
   of the human frame as the exaltation of human nature
   to the level of Godhead by its union with the Divine."
   (P. 32.)

Several inferences follow from the above statement:

a. In advaitic philosophy there is no two-way traffic. It is
only one way — from man to God. Hence by the realization of
his true nature, i.e., Brahman-Atman, man becomes divine. In
this there is no acceptance of limitation by the divine, but the
discarding of limitation by man to become divine. This is the
deification of man. In the Christological context this is the equivalent of " adoptionism."

b. There is not one incarnation but millions of incarnations,
and their significance is uniform. Hinduism, it must be noted, recognizes full, half, and quarter incarnations of God. Further by
the recognition of animal, half-animal–half-man, and human incarnations as equally significant and justified, the emphasis is
laid on the metaphysical immanence of God, which is indifferent
to the distinctions of tree, animal, and man. But does not man
get some special significance when it is said that the incarnations
take place in order to save good men?

2. " Theism, however, makes out that Kṛṣṇa is an incarnation (*avatāra*) or descent of the Divine into the human frame. Though the Lord knows no birth and

> change, He has many times been born." (P. 32.) " An
> *avātara* is a descent of God into man and not an ascent
> of man into God, which is the case with the liberated
> soul." (P. 34.)

This line of thought is quite the opposite of the previous. This
is more like the incarnation; the other is pure and simple deification. Let us see further what this incarnation means.

> " The assumption of human nature by the Divine Real-
> ity, like the creation of the world, does not take away from
> or add to the integrity of the Divine. Creation and incarna-
> tion both belong to the world of manifestation and not to
> the Absolute Spirit." (Pp. 32–33.)

The real question is: How can the Divine Reality create or assume human nature if there is no internal and eternal justification within it for doing so? To say that the creation and incarnation neither subtract from nor add anything to the Divine
Reality would mean that it is self-sufficient. This self-sufficiency
cannot be barren. On the other hand, it will imply an internal
and eternal inexhaustible richness of the being of God. This
richness cannot be chaotic but is internally ordered by the
Divine Wisdom. Thus to say that the Divine Reality creates
or assumes human nature, in other words, accepts external
limitation to manifest itself, will be meaningless, unless it implies that there is in the Divine Reality a ground for so doing —
that ground is indeed the self-limitation of God in his eternity.
Creation and incarnation may be said to belong to the " world
of manifestation " and not to the Absolute Spirit; but whose
manifestation is the " world of manifestation "? Are we going
to accept infinite regress or believe in " free creation "? The
difficulty with Radhakrishnan is that his view of the nature
of the Divine and hence of creation is defective. We invite him
to consider seriously the meaning of *creatio ex nihilo*.

> " If the Infinite God is manifested in finite existence
> throughout time, then Its special manifestation at one

given moment and through the assumption of one single human nature is but the free fulfillment of that same movement by which the Divine plentitude freely fulfills itself and inclines toward the finite. It does not raise any fresh problem apart from that of creation." (P. 33.)

No one denies that the possibility of an incarnation is dependent upon the possibility of creation. If God can create, i.e., if he can enter into relationship with the world at large, he can also affirm relationship with any particular item of his creation. So far we agree that the incarnation raises no special problem apart from the creation. On this premise there can be at least as many incarnations as there are individual entities in this world. One can even say that the incarnation is not necessary because creation is incarnation. But in all this there is an assumption that is quite unacceptable in the light of the facts of experience. Radhakrishnan himself is inclined to agree with us. The assumption is that a stone, a tree, a fish, a fowl, an animal, and a man are all equal in worth. What does he mean when he says that the relation between the Absolute and the finite human individual is "unimaginably intimate though difficult to define and explain" (p. 33)? Is it the same with regard to a stone or a tree, etc.? Again he says, "In the great souls we call incarnations, God who is responsible for the being and dignity of man has more wonderfully renewed it" (p. 33). Does this mean that a tree or a stone, etc., has dignity? What is the meaning of the "deeper sense" in which the divine is manifested in the human and not in any other cosmic element? If he is not merely playing with words, then the human incarnation raises a special problem of meaning and significance. This would mean that the most adequate incarnation of God can take place only at the human level. Thus the human level is quite distinct from the subhuman levels. When we say that only man can be the most adequate incarnation of God we concede in principle that every human individual has the possibility of being the incarnation. But whereas man is an abstraction, human individuals are not. They fall within cer-

tain historical traditions. Hence God can manifest himself most
adequately in the most responsive human personality in the
most adequate historical tradition. This can be none other than
Jesus Christ, the God-Man. There is no need of laboring the
point. This has been discussed by us in other places in the
book.

> "The fact of descent, or *avātara*, indicates that the Di-
> vine is not opposed to a full vital and physical manifesta-
> tion. . . . Human nature is not a fetter but can become an
> instrument of divine life." (Pp. 34, 35.) "Liberation is
> not the isolation of the immortal spirit from the mortal hu-
> man life but is the transfiguration of the whole man. . . .
> His [the saved one's] body, life, and mind are not dissolved
> but are rendered pure and become the means and mold of
> the Divine Light, and he becomes his own masterpiece.
> His personality is raised to its fullness, its maximum expres-
> sion, pure and free, buoyant and unburdened." (P. 76.)
> "Anchored in the timeless foundation of our spiritual exist-
> ence, the freed soul, the eternal individual works for the
> *jivaloka;* while possessing individuality of body, life, and
> mind he yet retains the universality of spirit." (P. 77.)
> "The freed spirits have no need for individuality but still
> assume it by self-limitation." (P. 77.)

These quotations are quite consistent with the spirit of theism.
Several inferences follow:

a. Human nature is not essentially opposed to God. There can
therefore be relationship between God and man which is called
the incarnation.

b. Because there is no opposition, human persons can have a
place in ultimate Reality and not be annihilated in any way.
Liberation is the liberation of the whole man.

c. As a foreshadowing of this ultimate state where the one
and the many will be reconciled, we have the saved souls who
still retain their individuality and work for the salvation of the

others. Their individuality is so reconciled to the spirit that it
does not involve them again in the karmic cycle. The meaning
of the resurrection of Jesus Christ is that the whole man is uplifted to the divine world. Salvation is for the total man. Just as
the spirit is redeemed, so is the body. Radhakrishnan misunder-
stands when he says: "The physical resurrection of Jesus is not
the important thing but the resurrection of the Divine" (p. 36).

3. "Though the Gita accepts the belief in *avātara,* as the
Divine limiting himself for some purpose on earth, pos-
sessing in his limited form the fullness of knowledge, it
also lays stress on the eternal *avātara,* the God in man,
the Divine consciousness always present in the human
being." (P. 35.)

Here one again begins to notice the retreat of Radhakrishnan
from theism toward absolute monism. The next quotation com-
pletes the retreat.

"When the Divine birth takes place within us, the scales
fall from our eyes, the bolts of the prison open. The Lord
abides in the heart of every creature and when the veil of
that secret sanctuary is withdrawn, we hear the Divine
voice, receive the Divine light, act in the Divine power. The
embodied human consciousness is uplifted into the unborn
eternal. The incarnation of Kṛṣṇa is not so much the conver-
sion of Godhead into flesh as the taking up of manhood
into God." (P. 36.)

Hence Radhakrishnan abandons the theistic view of the "descent" of God into man, and accepts the monistic view of a
mere "ascent" of man into God. And one is left wondering
what drives him away from theism to absolute monism.[77]

VII

THE NEW ADAM

Contemporary man has need of a different kind of asceticism, of concentration, of renunciation, of a limitation of growing necessities and their infinite longing. The foundations must be laid of this new asceticism as well as of a new spirituality. The ontological justification of asceticism is its achievement of simplicity or wholeness, of freedom from complexity or disintegration. But the achievement of divine simplicity implies not the annihilation of the complex world, but its illumination and transfiguration, its integration in a higher unity. This involves the appearance of a new type of saint, who will take upon himself the burden of the complex world. (*Spirit and Reality,* by Nicolas Berdyaev, p. 99.)

THE CONQUEST OF SIN AND ANXIETY BY JESUS CHRIST AND THE APPEARANCE OF NEW HUMANITY

IT IS THE EXPLICIT as well as the implicit conviction of the New Testament writers that in Jesus Christ has been revealed a hitherto undisclosed dimension of truth and meaning concerning the relation between God and man. A new being has appeared, providing thereby a possibility for man to be man. Such a possibility is made possible because the new being comprises the dimension of divinity as well as of humanity. Paul calls this new being the " Second Adam " — the Risen Christ. The Christ is the New Creation as well as the basis of it. New Humanity takes its

174

birth from him. In him grace and truth have come into being.

The moment such statements are made, deep and disturbing questions arise. How is such a phenomenon possible in the context of sinful history? Some might assert that such a question is irrelevant. They argue that God is the God of this world and this world belongs to him. He is related to the world, and there should not be any hindrance between God, man, and the world. So far there is no disagreement, for it cannot be denied that the world at no time ceases to be God's world. But if it is argued further that on the religio-moral level there exists also the same kind of relation of immanence and providence, then it is to be denied. The theories that presuppose such a conception mainly fall into two categories. One view sees the relation from the human side. The spiritual and moral life of man supported by the notion of progress advances with rapid strides, and the net result of such a progression is at one point or another the deification of man. He becomes the measure of all things. Such a view does not realize that the religio-moral situation of man is much more complex than to receive its solution only from the idea of progress. The tragedies of our life and civilization have brought before our eyes the naked fact that not only progress but retrogression is also a profound reality of our life. The whole position is based on the essential goodness of man. And once that basis is given and some encumbrances have been removed, it naturally culminates in the attainment of divinity. Such a view is an extreme simplification, and is an unjustifiable equation of the technical achievements of man with his religious and moral life. The latter is not governed by the same law of horizontal development as the former.

The other view looks at the world from the standpoint of God. The immanent presence of God according to this view pervades everything. Nothing is impervious to his presence. He is equally present everywhere, and if there are differences they are insignificant. Such differences can be overcome by some effort and discipline. One has only to turn to any part of the world to find that God is there. So the movements incorporating the idea of " back to nature " find their inspiration in such sources. Such a view also is an oversimplification. It does not realize that the religio-moral life of man can banish the presence of God out of its consciousness in such a way that it does not play any conscious part in molding or directing it. The truth in the position, however, is that such a life still continues, and it is so because of the sustaining presence of God. This truth is not contested. What is objected to is the nondifference between the presence of God as it is related to, say, a tree and as it is related to the spiritual-ethical consciousness of man. This theory also treats personality and history in a trivial way. According to it, personality and history are only temporary modes of manifestation.

Both these views regard the surd in history rather lightly, and a Christology constructed according to these patterns yields nothing but a caricature. A true Christology must face the question of sin in history. This means that the humanity of Jesus Christ cannot be impersonal or ideal. It is actual. It is the humanity of a historical personality participating in the complexities of historicosocial living. His humanity cannot be abstracted from its relations without distortion. However noble the aim may be, such a procedure is unwarranted.

The New Testament makes two statements about Jesus Christ. The first statement depicts him as involved in the stream of historical, sinful humanity. He is tempted all through his life. He is born in the likeness of sinful flesh. The second statement, and this statement is more implicit than explicit, bears witness to the fact that, despite the truth of the first statement, he never succumbed to actual sin. The truth of the matter does not consist in either of these statements taken singly, but in their interrelation and the situation that this interrelation creates and encompasses.

Jesus Christ as a historical person comes in the line of created and procreated humanity. He cannot be abstracted from this context except by an arbitrary act. This act may mean that, irrespective of the concreteness of humanity within which he appears, his is a pure and ideal humanity. It is hard to be reconciled to such an arbitrariness. It deprives Jesus Christ of solidarity with the rest of mankind. We should, therefore, look at the question from another angle. Jesus Christ is related to the past of mankind. He is in part the creation of that past. As an individual he stands surrounded by the accumulated sins of human beings. In this respect he does not stand before history but within history. He shares the locus within sinful history with other men. He identifies himself with sinful men within sinful history. Whether he further identifies himself with men by committing sin and thereby making the burden of history more burdensome remains to be seen.

Let us in brief see our own position in history. I, as an individual, am related to historical humanity in two ways. First, I stand in the nexus of history and, secondly, I am surrounded by the sins of others to which I add my own, creating thereby a larger accumulation of sins for generations to come. However, I do not add my sin to the others as a matter of necessity. There is no irrevocable law forcing me to do so. There are external as well as internal conditions that make my sinning possible. But the doing of it is a result of my own decision. The external condition that facilitates my sinful act is the sinful state that affects and pervades history. The internal condition is the anxiety of my total inward existence. It is inextricably tied up with the polarity of my existence. One pole pulls me toward my past, toward the devouring forces of the unconscious realm of tradition and nature; the other pole, toward boundless creativity and the inexhaustible realm of possibilities. If I succumb to the lures of the former, I cease to be a human being. I lose my freedom. To fall into the coils of the second is to pronounce myself as the infinite and the absolute. By that I also lose my freedom and fall prey to the demonic forces. I must remain a human being, for in that lies my destiny. And the extent of my success would reflect the measure of the fulfillment of my destiny.

Anxiety is the state of inward existence which has "nothingness" as its object. It is an existence between freedom and necessity, spirit and nature, and finitude and infinity. But the moment

anxiety has "something" as its object it has become fear, and
struggle has begun to overcome this fear. Sin has already posited
itself. Thus by the conspiracy by which the pervasive sinfulness
enters into relation with my internal anxiety personal sin is committed. This is, in a few words, the story of the historical man.

However, a question may very legitimately be raised at this
point. How and why does the "first human being" fall prey to
sinfulness? This question really does not have much force except that it clears a certain confusion. The answer is that, although sin and freedom are in no way identical, the possibility
of sin is implied in finite freedom. Similarly, goodness and freedom are not identical, but the possibility of being good is present in man's freedom. Sin in this respect is a presupposition of
history. What is meant by this statement is that the origin of sin
cannot be traced back to any chronological beginning. It is part
of the mystery of man. In this mystery the "first human being"
has no precedence over the later ones. Chronology is out of
place here.

The most crucial question to be answered is, How did Jesus
Christ become an exception to sinfulness? It is said that he was
tempted like us in all points and yet did not succumb. How is it
possible?

The answer to this question lies in the self-consciousness of Jesus Christ. The problem of the self-consciousness of Jesus is a
very controversial issue among New Testament scholars of note.
Our study of the New Testament materials has made that point
clear. The position put forth in these pages is that Jesus was conscious of his being the Suffering Servant of God and the exalted
Son of Man. It is also made clear that such a consciousness became explicit at baptism. It means that the anxiety in Jesus
which is the fate of all human beings was conquered by the presence of God in him and by his being rooted and grounded in
God. But this does not mean that anxiety was overcome entirely
at once. On the contrary, it is only a beginning. The tremendous
temptations that stormed the inner citadel of his being did not
let him rest to the very last days of his life. This only goes to

show how incredibly strenuous and painful the struggle was against the lure of extremely subtle enslavements. As he grew more in the knowledge of God the temptations increased their fury, but the corresponding conquest of anxiety was also consolidated more and more. The battle proceeds on such a tremendous and unimaginable scale that it is impossible to gauge the magnitude of its depth and power.

Finally the battle is brought to a final crisis. The alternative was, as always, to forsake God and to elevate finite elements of existence to the position of the " Highest " Reality. The choice was either to sin or to die. Jesus Christ chose the latter. The cross is the symbol of the complete conquest of anxiety and contingency of human existence by the love and trust in God. The resurrection is the autograph of God to that effect. The true security that is the conquest of anxiety comes not by saving but by losing oneself. That is the meaning of the life of Jesus Christ from the beginning to its very end. The losing is rendering impotent any element of finite personal existence to rise and declare itself in its own right as absolute and unconditioned.

There is, therefore, in Jesus Christ the perfect union between God and man which has no sign or taint of law and necessity but is through and through informed by grace and love, trust and obedience. In him God and man are reconciled. Jesus Christ is the reconciliation. The meaning of this reconciliation is that in him divine-humanity has come to be a fact. Essential humanity, which bears the *imago Dei,* or essential God-manhood, has become real in him. In him God and man have become identified though not identical. The purpose of God, the destiny of man, have been both disclosed and fulfilled in him.

The essential structure of creation becomes manifest. The very creation of the " cosmos " betrays the prejudice of God toward order and goodness. But, because God is the creator and not the cause of the cosmos, the order and the goodness cannot be maintained and created by force and necessity. The God who is a cause of the cosmos rules out by causal necessity any and every chaos, but God who is the creator respects the freedom of the created man and does not rule out the possibility of chaos and disobedience. He recognizes man's freedom and overcomes rebellion by love and grace. The intention of God for the world has been realized through Jesus Christ by means of love and grace.

How is it then, someone may object, that the world still continues to sin? Has not the sinful world come to an end in Jesus Christ? The objection is based on the principle of causality. If the sinful world were a causal order and the wills of all men were identical with the will of one man, such a happening would immediately bring about the end of the causal series. The world on that premise should have come to an end. But in a strictly causal nexus how could such an event take place? Moreover, why should such an event take place when what is either good or bad or both is due to necessity?

The truth of the matter is that sin is due to freedom, and in spite of the appearance of divine-humanity people can still go on sinning if they so decide. There is, however, one fundamental difference, and that consists in the fact that divine-humanity has cut the deepest roots of sin. It means that the source of power has been disclosed, and the possibility has been created whereby men, by affirming their relationship to that source and by availing themselves of the possibility, can carry on a winning struggle against sin in themselves and in society.

This is first and foremost achieved in the total life of a man through perfect obedience and trust. But this man is not an isolated man. He is also the representative man. The new humanity has appeared in him in a corporate way. This is not, however, to argue for a kind of platonic realism that understands by corporate humanity the real and individual presence of every human being. On the contrary, it means that although every human individual would be able to overcome the contradiction in his being if he would voluntarily affirm his relationship with Jesus Christ, yet the very possibility that would enable him to do so is already there to be taken advantage of.

There is something more. The individual who endeavors to overcome the sinfulness of his situation is already helped along that way because someone else has already overcome sin. Moreover, the Spirit of God constantly inspires the striving soul. The disclosure of the source of power and the possibility and corresponding human willingness and decision to avail oneself of the source and the possibility creates the *koinōnia,* the blessed fellowship. The fellowship is created by God's taking hold of the human soul and its voluntary response to it. The fellowship is one of the most potent categories of New Testament thought and life.

The immediate fellowship of disciples was created by the call of Jesus and the response of those who were called. Within this fellowship they learned by rare intimacy the mystery of the person of the Lord. However, it was not till after the resurrection experience and the active indwelling of the Holy Spirit that they began to know the ultimate mystery of his being. The knowledge of the Master's Person was existential knowledge. It could be learned only by living in fellowship with him and with others who also desired communion with him. The path of such a fellowship is neither simple nor easy. It is difficult and demands all the resources of men and even more. In fact, it can be made possible only through God.

THE RECONCILIATION OF SINFUL HUMANITY AND THE WORLD AT LARGE

The follower of Jesus Christ has to walk in the footsteps of the Master. In the language of Paul, he has to be baptized, crucified, buried, and resurrected with him. This does not mean that one should follow the known course of Jesus' life in a literal fashion. However, the essential truth has to be lived. One has to bear the cross and save one's life by losing it. There is no other way.

In this fellowship men are restored to wholeness, they find meaning in life, and their fragmentary life and outlook receive greater integration. They become reconciled with God, with themselves, and with others. We should not, however, labor under any illusions about the degree of this reconciliation. We can be easily duped by plausible perfectionisms and utopian day-dreaming. The conflicts of personal life, the realities of day-to-day living, and the periodic upheavals of world-shaking magnitude should bar us from slipping into a facile optimism. The battle of overcoming the sinfulness of history will last till the very end of history. But this does not imply that we should thereby resign ourselves to a philosophy of despair and grim pessimism. Such neat alternatives are no longer possible. The situation in history from one point of view has become more complex.

Let us see where we stand so far. In Jesus Christ, God and man are reconciled. Sin in history has been conquered on the cross. The truth is made patent that in Jesus Christ all things cohere. He is the basis of all reconciliation and coherence in all levels where God, man, and the world touch and are related to one another. Within the fellowship of those who love and obey him reconciliation takes place between an individual and his God and his fellow man. But from this it should not be concluded that sin has been eliminated from history. It only means that now we have power and precedence on our side by which a hard, realistic, and on the whole, winning battle can be fought against the concerted conspiracy of the forces of evil. We are now enabled in such a way that if we put ourselves at the disposal of the vision granted us we can significantly affect the course of human life and society toward their proper fulfillment.

The principle of reconciliation should be extended beyond the society of men. It should be carried to the very heart of the world of things and nature. The outlook of man informed by the basic experience of reconciliation should manipulate the world of nature, the animals and the things therein in such a way that nothing that God has created is shut out from the restoration and fulfillment of the destiny of the cosmos which is God's purpose for it. The apostle Paul says that the whole creation groans for the day of the liberty of the sons of God, for its liberation is tied up with theirs, just as its subjection to sin is also the result of the sinfulness of man. Man must be reconciled to nature and the things of nature.

In the historical, cultural, and religious situation of the world the same fellowship that was later enlarged and called by the name "ecclesia" was entrusted with the message of reconciliation. Within the church the Lord of the church is present constantly through his indwelling Spirit. That is how the church launched out into the deep and still carries on the universal and ecumenical ministry of healing the wounds of sick and divided men and reconciling them to God, themselves, their fellow men, and their world. When the church deviates from this high purpose it loses its place of effectiveness in the world and betrays its Lord and Master. The history of the church as an organization is all too full of such betrayals. In spite of all these failures it is nonetheless the peculiar privilege of the church as the communion of the beloved and the faithful to be the earnest of the Kingdom of God in the midst of history.

THE TENDENCY TOWARD DISTORTED RECONCILIATION PRESENT IN OTHER RELIGIOUS AND SECULAR AND TECHNICAL SPHERES

Is the religious history of the non-Christian world devoid of an attempt at such a reconciliation? At the very outset it should be acknowledged that the various forms of historical Christianity have been anything but a reconciliation. It is as if the forces of evil, secularization, and objectivization have attacked the church with such fury that the vision of its reconciling ministry has been obscured, dulled and beclouded from time to time. The quest of all religions is after God. Every religion aims at union with what it conceives to be the highest and central reality. This basic urge, which is the characteristic mark of all true religion, has created for its realization various forms of religions, ranging from crude animatism and asceticism to the most refined types of mysticism such as the Hindu advaitism (as represented by Śankara) and Neoplatonism. True spirituality and genuine reconciliation safeguard personality, freedom, and love. Any form of reconciliation that obscures any of these is indeed distorted. In Radhakrishnan we have seen that, in spite of his professions of concrete monism, he has in the last resort submerged the plural world of personality into the undifferentiated abyss of the Absolute. It is only Christian reconciliation that safeguards personality, freedom, and love. And this is true in spite of the many distortions of churches and church councils.

There is then in the non-Christian religions a genuine element of truth. Moreover, there are heroic examples of living out this truth in life and thought. Such lives and their achievements are to be neither underestimated nor neglected. They are the allies of the Christian truth. They are the children of the Christ. They will find their proper fulfillment and criticism in Jesus Christ. Such souls are in the vanguard for the battle against evil and sin. It is because of them that the Christ is expected, and it is because they cannot create the Christ that the Christ comes. Jesus Christ is, therefore, the fulfillment and judgment of the Hebraic-prophetic tradition as well as of other religious traditions. He appears in the Hebraic-prophetic tradition because it of all traditions was most capable of receiving him. Jesus Christ is not an accident in the life of Hebrew religion and thought, although even it could not produce the Christ. The Christ comes.

Not only religions, but systems of economics, politics, and culture are also attempts at the harmonization of man with himself and his environment. Like religion these systems embody important truth in so far as they want to rescue man and reconcile him to the best that is possible. However, in the concrete and actual working out of this truth the result has been the dehumanization of man. This is particularly true of bourgeois capitalism. It arose as a protest against the feudalistic economy that suppressed the individual. Its purpose was to save the human person and provide him with opportunities of realizing his potentialities to the full. It has ended in respecting only the personality of a few, and has turned the mass of humanity into nothing but robots and commodities. Socialism, which protests against capitalism and wants to free man from the tyranny of money and bring him closer to existential realities, would serve well, if it does not impose upon the individual the tyranny of the mass. But that is just what has happened in many systems of socialistic economy.

In the systems of political democracy and totalitarianisms the same principle holds. Since the largest democracies have capitalistic economies, they recognize the theoretical right of every individual to be himself in the complete sense of the term, but practically most of the population lives a robot existence. Moreover, in democracies the individual becomes much more rationalistic and therefore individualistic in a rather bad sense of that word. He loses the capacity for true society and fellowship. The present breakdown of the family in such societies is an illustration of the point.

In the totalitarian systems of all types the individual does not exist. It is some corporate entity, the state, race, or the proletariat, that constitutes the living reality. This is a return to the elemental forces of unconscious nature. The individual is absorbed and no more remains self-identical.

The Renaissance culture discovered the individual. It set him against the world and gave him the tools to conquer the forces of nature. Man was conceived as essentially good and full of creative possibilities. The question was not the reconciliation of man to his environment, but of all things to man. So a completely autonomous culture was built. In it man and his environment were reconciled. But the reconciliation was too intellectualistic and did not take note of the irrational elements in man. Under the urge of the elemental forces in man this partial, intellectualistic, and moralistic culture broke down. The Renaissance analysis of the human situation was only partial, and that weakness resulted in its final breakdown.

The romantic reaction led to all kinds of aesthetic attempts at harmonization. These attempts may be conveniently divided into two kinds. Both are mystical. One type of mysticism endeavors to discover the deep underlying principle of harmony which is present in the deepest reaches of both man and nature. By some kind of artistic, aesthetic, and mystical activity this harmony is realized. The harmony, however, results in the absorption of the individual into the all-pervading principle of harmony, call it God or something else.

The other is a vitalistic type of mysticism. This is a return to nature of the prereflective stage. By allowing oneself to be taken into the dance of the elemental urges of the forces of nature one is saved from a solitary, individualistic existence. Here the individual also falls prey to the Dionysian forces and loses himself. The romantic reaction also deals with the partial man and thinks that it is dealing with the whole man.

Of late the psychoanalytical method has tried to cure people of their illusions and heal their psychological ailments. But it is not capable of dealing with the total depth of man. Berdyaev observes: " The psychoanalytical method claims to free the consciousness from illusions and psychological traumas, but it is not a spiritual method. Spirituality cannot be merely psychoanalysis; it must necessarily be psychosynthesis."

THREE STAGES IN THE STORY OF THE HUMAN SPIRIT

New Testament thought recognizes three stages in the story of the human spirit. The first stage is of a kind of paradisiacal innocence. Man is in close harmony with nature and the process of individuation or differentiation has not started yet. He is so caught up in the vitalities surrounding him that he is an obedient child of nature. He knows life more instinctively, and his intuition is more of a natural sort.

This immediacy of life and outlook is broken through by his anxiety, freedom, and desire to know. His limitless possibilities clamor for expression. In the act of such transcendence man both falls and rises. He falls from his blissful and simple existence; he rises because he knows himself in contradistinction to nature, in whose bosom he once innocently played and slept. He reflects, reasons, and decides. In all this he has sinned, in so far as he turned the glory of the incorruptible God into the image of mortal man. He falls under the law. The law convicts him as well as gives him the opportunity to conform to the law. His attempts at conformity to the law result in legalistic righteousness. Such righteousness fans the egotism of the so-called righteous and makes him more and more self-righteous and self-sufficient. This lands man in a vicious circle, for by the law man cannot save himself.

It is grace and faith that rescue man. The Spirit of God groans with the spirit of man. The working of God is neither like the unconscious nature, nor like legalisms that imprison man's freedom. The grace of God works from within; it enlightens from inside. The freedom of man is respected. However, in the relation of grace and freedom the human individual is affirmed as well as denied. He is unconditionally affirmed as the child and image of God, and he is denied because grace-informing freedom takes away from freedom its inordinate love of itself and its desire to establish itself in the place of the highest. The New Testament declares that this happens in and through Jesus Christ. The state of being " in Christ," where the quality of personal integrity is unconditionally affirmed and the quality of intrapersonal relatedness is achieved to the highest degree, is the most enriched state of existence. The truth of other stages is not denied but fulfilled. Man is guided by an inward spirit and is reconciled to his total environment.

The same stages can be described in terms that sound more psychological. These stages respectively are unconsciousness, consciousness, and superconsciousness. From the immediacy and intuition of nature, through reason and law, to " mystical " intuition and faith, life is infinitely enriched. These stages are by no means chronological, and an individual may find himself entangled in them very unchronologically.

THE NEW CREATION AND HIS IMPACT ON THE ENVIRONMENT

The point is that a new creature comes into being; he is the integral man — that is, the man who stands in a relationship of creative union and fellowship with God, himself, other men, and nature. Such an individual is always in the making; he seems never to have become a finished product. His wholeness or integrality seems to remain always partial, but receives greater and greater co-ordination as he persists in his basic relationships. There is no automatic law of progress. It is a very difficult task. The ideal is the man born out of the impact of eternity and history who would feel, act, and know himself to be himself in the vast and intricate network of unbounded interrelationships. However, for the proximate ends in history we need men whose lives would reflect more and more coherence, wholeness, and integrality in their impact upon the whole world. It is needless to say that psychology cannot deal with the situation adequately. Its help is and must be accepted. But for issues that lie deeper than psychology, deeper resources have to be drawn upon.

By the appearance of the new creature the sharpest conflicts in history arise. A situation of inconceivable tension gives rise to endless dualisms. The forces of evil put up the strongest front, and every inch of territory is to be won by stubborn resistance. The individual who lives *sub specie aeternitatis* and *sub specie temporis* has no exclusive, clear-cut panaceas. His citizenship in the eternal realm while being caught up in the trammels of historical temporality can be affirmed only by taking up the cross every day. But for the grace of God man's situation becomes endless misery and despair.

History cannot be reversed. The Christ has come. We are no more confronted with a philosophy of despair. Sheer optimism is strongly tempered with hard realism. The ground for ultimate victory has appeared. Resources of power have been disclosed. If we willingly appropriate and intentionally surrender, the cosmos can be redeemed and reconciled by the paradox that dying is living and grasping at life is to die. We are not in the fight alone; God is with us.

In so far as an individual is reconciled in his basic relationship (and such a reconciliation is a matter of everyday life, of all life and even beyond) his manifold activities begin to bear the imprint of coherence. His various pursuits — economic, political, artistic, technical, and others — do not stand isolated and in conscious hostility, but they are creatively interwoven without losing their separate identity and yet making constructive modifications and contributions toward the well-rounded development one of another. Much of the life of modern man is shot through and through with glaring contradictions, absurdities, and divisions. His house is terribly divided against itself. Only a radical cure can heal his radical malady. Let us take an instance.

The modern university is a symbol of spatial unity. The sciences taught stand in a relation of juxtaposition. It is easy to see that for scientific discovery and for the development of new sciences a certain amount of autonomy is a prerequisite, but it does not follow that their autonomy should breed a creed of isolationism. It is not quite conceivable why the activities of man should be so isolated from one another unless there is something radically wrong with him. It cannot, therefore, be overstressed that it is the integral man who can give coherence to these sciences. None of the externally imposed unities or uniformities can ever do for that integral pattern which the genius of a reconciled man can weave into the very texture of his creations. The modern university needs a soul. Its center is missing. It is the genius of the whole man which can animate the dried body of its sciences.

Much of what has been said above remains an ideal. But a real ground exists in history for the pursuit of the ideal. The history of the church and of the non-Christian religions can to an extent justify the approximation to the ideal. The Kingdom of God is present in our midst although it is still not here in power. We should live heroically and sacrificially by and in the light of the New Adam, to the end that all may be subsumed under him and we be subjected to God so that God be all and in all. This is not the submergence of the plural world of persons, but on the contrary, the union of God, man, and the world. It is the affirmation of the cosmos.

" And He Himself appointed some to be apostles, some to be

prophets, some to be evangelists, some to be pastors and teach-
ers, in order fully to equip His people for the work of serving —
for the building up of Christ's body — till we all of us arrive at
oneness in faith and in the knowledge of the Son of God, and at
mature manhood and the stature of full-grown men in Christ."

NOTES

Chapter I. Light on Christian Origins

1. Thomas W. Manson, *The Servant-Messiah* (Cambridge University Press, Cambridge, 1953), pp. 19 ff.

2. Oscar Cullmann, *The Christology of the New Testament*, tr. by Shirley C. Guthrie and Charles A. M. Hall (The Westminster Press, 1959), p. 166.

3. Millar Burrows, *The Dead Sea Scrolls* (The Viking Press, Inc., 1955), p. 327.

4. Millar Burrows, *More Light on the Dead Sea Scrolls* (The Viking Press, Inc., 1958), pp. 39 ff.

5. Charles H. Dodd, *The Bible and the Greeks* (Alec R. Allenson, Inc., 1954), p. 247.

6. Robert M. Grant, *Gnosticism and Early Christianity* (Columbia University Press, 1959), pp. 34 ff.

7. Hans Jonas, *The Gnostic Religion,* (The Beacon Press, Inc., 1958), p. xvi.

8. Krister Stendahl, ed., *The Scrolls and the New Testament* (Harper & Brothers, 1957), p. 30.

9. Cullmann, *The Christology of the New Testament*, p. 165.

10. Cullmann, *The Early Church*, tr. by A. J. B. Higgins (The Westminster Press, 1954), p. 186.

11. William Manson, *The Epistle to the Hebrews* (Hodder & Stoughton, Ltd., London, 1951), p. 31.

12. Martin Dibelius, *Studies in the Acts of the Apostles* (Charles Scribner's Sons, 1956), p. 126.

13. Albert Schweitzer, *The Quest of the Historical Jesus* (The Macmillan Company, 1948), p. 349.

191

14. *Ibid.*, p. 357.

15. *Ibid.*, p. 358.

16. Dodd, *The Apostolic Preaching and Its Developments* (Harper & Brothers, 1936), p. 147.

17. *Ibid.*, p. 84.

18. Dodd, *The Coming of Christ* (Cambridge University Press, Cambridge, 1951), pp. 16–18.

19. Dodd, *The Apostolic Preaching and Its Developments*, p. 167.

20. Dodd, *The Coming of Christ*, pp. 15, 16.

21. Dodd, *The Interpretation of the Fourth Gospel* (Cambridge University Press, Cambridge, 1953), p. 447.

22. Rudolf Bultmann, *Theology of the New Testament* (Charles Scribner's Sons, 1954), Vol. I, p. 9.

23. *Ibid.*, p. 21.

24. *Ibid.*, pp. 25, 26.

25. Werner Georg Kümmel, *Promise and Fulfilment: The Eschatological Message of Jesus,* tr. by Dorothea M. Barton (Alec R. Allenson, Inc., 1957), p. 155.

26. Dodd, *New Testament Studies* (Charles Scribner's Sons, 1952), p. 11.

27. Matthew Black, *An Aramaic Approach to the Gospels and Acts* (Oxford University Press, Inc., 1954), pp. 7, 12.

28. *Ibid.*, p. 206.

CHAPTER II. The Divinity of Jesus Christ

1. William Sanday and A. C. Headlam, *The Epistle to the Romans* (International Critical Commentary) (Charles Scribner's Sons), p. 238.

2. Dodd, *The Epistle of Paul to the Romans* (Moffatt New Testament Commentary) (Harper & Brothers, 1932), p. 152.

3. *Ibid.*, p. 152.

4. J. H. Michael, *The Epistle of Paul to the Philippians* (Moffatt N. T. Com.) (Harper & Brothers, 1927), p. 84.

5. Ernest F. Scott, *The Epistle of Paul to the Colossians, etc.,* (Moffatt N. T. Com.) (Harper & Brothers, 1930), p. 20.

6. James Moffatt, *The First Epistle of Paul to the Corinthians* (Moffatt N. T. Com.) (Harper & Brothers, 1938), p. 251.

7. Theodore H. Robinson, *The Epistle to the Hebrews* (Moffatt N. T. Com.) (Harper & Brothers, 1933), p. xvi.

8. Ernest F. Scott, *The Epistle to the Hebrews* (T. & T. Clark, Edinburgh, 1923), p. 156.

9. James Moffatt, *The Epistle to the Hebrews* (Int. Crit. Com.) (Charles Scribner's Sons), p. 6.

10. Alfred E. J. Rawlinson, *The New Testament Doctrine of the Christ* (Longmans, Green & Co., Inc., 1949), p. 187.

11. E. F. Scott, *The Epistle to the Hebrews*, p. 164.

12. Brooke F. Westcott, ed., *The Epistle to the Hebrews* (Wm. B. Eerdmans Publishing Company, 1950), p. 410.

13. Moffatt, *The Epistle to the Hebrews* (Int. Crit. Com.), pp. 6, 7.

14. Mark 8:27-30; Luke 9:18-21; Matt. 16:13-20; John 6:66-69.

15. Prof. Frederick C. Grant, discussing Mark's conception of the Messianic Secret, says, "It is subsidiary to his whole interpretation of the life of Jesus as already Messiah while upon earth, and long before his resurrection" in *The Earliest Gospel* (Abingdon Press, 1943), p. 161.

16. G. Dalman, *The Words of Jesus* (T. & T. Clark, Edinburgh, 1907), pp. 237, 238.

17. *Ibid.*, p. 249.

18. Rudolf Otto, *The Kingdom of God and the Son of Man* (Lutterworth Press, London, 1943), p. 248; W. Manson, *Jesus the Messiah* (The Beacon Press, Inc., 1957), p. 117.

19. Frederick John Foakes-Jackson and Kirsopp Lake, eds., *The Beginnings of Christianity* (The Macmillan Company, 1920), Vol. I, p. 373.

20. Dalman, *op. cit.*, p. 250.

21. Foakes-Jackson and Lake, *op. cit.*, Vol. I, pp. 374, 370 ff.

22. Discussed in Vincent Taylor, *Jesus and His Sacrifice* (The Macmillan Company, 1937), pp. 25–26; Vincent Taylor, *The Gospel According to St. Mark* (Macmillan & Co., Ltd., London, 1952), pp. 197–200.

23. Otto, *op. cit.*, p. 213.

24. Taylor, *Jesus and His Sacrifice*, pp. 24–26.

25. *Ibid.*

26. T. W. Manson, *The Teaching of Jesus* (Cambridge University Press, Cambridge, 1935), pp. 227, 212.

27. Foakes-Jackson and Lake, *op. cit.*, Vol. I, p. 370.

28. T. W. Manson, *The Teaching of Jesus,* pp. 227–228.

29. *Ibid.*, p. 90; Dalman, *op. cit.*, pp. 272, 273.

30. Mark 1:11; Luke 3:22; Matt. 3:17.

31. Mark 9:7; Luke 9:35; Matt. 17:5.

32. Foakes-Jackson and Lake, *op. cit.*, Vol. I, p. 399.

33. T. W. Manson, *The Teaching of Jesus,* pp. 103, 104; Dalman, *op. cit.*, p. 280.

34. Matt. 11:11-13; Luke 7:28.

35. Taylor, *Jesus and His Sacrifice,* p. 38.

36. Dalman, *op. cit.*, p. 297.

37. Mark 1:1; 8:29; 9:41; 14:61; 15:32; 12:35; 13:21.

38. For the name, Acts 2:38; 3:6; 4:10; 9:34; 10:48; 11:17; 15:26; 16:18; 24:24; 28:31. For the title, Acts 2:36; 3:18; 3:20; 9:22; 17:3; 18:5; 18:28; 26:23.

39. Dalman, *op. cit.*, pp. 303, 304.

40. Foakes-Jackson and Lake, *op. cit.*, Vol. I, p. 416.

41. Dalman, *op. cit.*, pp. 330–331.

42. R. Harris, *The Origin of the Prologue to St. John* (Cambridge University Press, Cambridge, 1917), p. 30.

43. C. F. Burney, *The Aramaic Origin of the Fourth Gospel* (Clarendon Press, Oxford, 1922), p. 42.

44. *Ibid.*, p. 38.

45. George Foot Moore, *Judaism* (Harvard University Press, 1927), Vol. I, pp. 417 ff.

46. *Ibid.*

47. Robert H. Strachan, *The Fourth Gospel* (The Macmillan Company, 1942), p. 93.

48. Herbert Danby, ed. and tr., *Mishnah* (Oxford University Press, Inc., 1933), Sanhedrin 10:1; Aboth 3:15, 1:2.

49. J. H. Bernard, *St. John* (Int. Crit. Com.) (Charles Scribner's Sons, 1929), Vol. I, p. 13.

50. James Drummond, *Philo-Judeaus* (Williams and Norgate, London, 1888), p. 127.

51. Harry A. Wolfson, *Philo* (Harvard University Press, 1947), Vol. I, pp. 230–234.

52. *Ibid.*, p. 237.

53. G. H. C. Macgregor, *The Gospel of John* (Moffatt N. T. Com.) (Harper & Brothers, 1928), p. 5.

54. William Temple, *Readings in St. John's Gospel* (First Series) (The Macmillan Company, 1939–1940), pp. 12, 13.

55. Burney, *op. cit.*, pp. 34, 35.

56. Macgregor, *op. cit.*, p. 15.

57. John 10:30–38; 14:9–11.

58. John 3:35; 17:10; 4:34.

59. John 5:30; 6:38-39; 8:26; 10:18; 12:49; 14:31; 15:10.

60. The words are Paul's, but the experience is common to all disciples.

61. Ps. 2:7; Heb. 1:5; Acts 13:33.

CHAPTER III. The Humanity of Jesus Christ

1. The English school of scholars believes that the rediscovery of the historical Jesus was one of the specific aims of form criticism. See Edwin Basil Redlich, *Form Criticism* (Alec R. Allenson, Inc., 1948), pp. 11, 12; Vincent Taylor, *The Gospels* (Alec R. Allenson, Inc., 1956), p. 16. Even Bultmannian scholars are moving in this direction.

2. Charles A. Scott, *Christianity According to St. Paul* (Cambridge University Press, Cambridge, 1939), p. 12, and *Living Issues in the New Testament* (The Macmillan Company, 1933), p. 15.

3. Maurice Goguel, *Jesus the Nazarene (Myth or History?)*, tr. by Frederick Stephens (D. Appleton & Co., 1926), pp. 95, 96.

4. C. A. Scott, *Living Issues in the New Testament*, p. 18.

5. Rawlinson, *op. cit.*, p. 116.

6. C. A. Scott, *Living Issues in the New Testament*, p. 17. Cf. Rom. 15:8.

7. Bishop J. B. Lightfoot, *Commentary on Galatians* (Macmillan & Co., Ltd., London, 1892), p. 168.

8. G. O. Griffith, *St. Paul's Life of Christ* (G. H. Doran & Co.), p. 105; Phil. 2:8.

9. C. A. Scott, *Christianity According to St. Paul*, p. 125.

10. *Ibid.*, p. 14.

11. *Ibid.*, p. 15; Rom. 15:2.

12. Moffatt, *The Epistle to the Hebrews* (Int. Crit. Com.), p. 235.

13. B. F. Westcott, *op. cit.*, pp. 106, 107.

14. Moffatt, *The Epistle to the Hebrews* (Int. Crit. Com.), p. 59.

15. Westcott, *op. cit.*, p. 107.

16. Moffatt, *The Epistle to the Hebrews* (Int. Crit. Com.), p. 59.

17. For a detailed treatment, consult Vincent Taylor, *The Historical Evidence for the Virgin Birth* (Clarendon Press, Oxford, 1920).

18. Luke 2:25 ff. (The account is not quite clear.)

19. John Martin Creed, ed., *The Gospel According to St. Luke* (The Macmillan Company, 1930), pp. 43, 44.

20. Mark 1:9; Luke 3:21; Matt. 3:14, 16.

21. Mark 1:13; Luke 4:1–13; Matt. 4:1–10.

22. Maurice Goguel, *Life of Jesus,* tr. by Olive Wyon (The Macmillan Company, 1933), pp. 280, 281.

23. Luke 4:22. (Moffatt translates "gracious words.")

24. Claude J. G. Montefiore, *The Synoptic Gospels* (The Macmillan Company, 1927), Vol. II, p. 397.

25. *Ibid.,* p. 397.

26. John Wick Bowman, *The Intention of Jesus* (The Westminster Press, 1943), pp. 93 ff.

27. Luke 4:30; Otto Borchert, *The Original Jesus,* tr. by L. M. Stalker, ed. by R. Mercer Wilson (The Macmillan Company, 1933), p. 160.

28. C. F. Burney, *The Poetry of Our Lord* (Clarendon Press, Oxford, 1925).

29. Bishop Robert Lowth, *Isaiah: A New Translation* (Lackington, Hughes & Co., London, 1822), Vol. I, pp. xiv, xv; Bishop Robert Lowth, *The Sacred Poetry of the Hebrews* (Codman Press, Andover, 1878), pp. 210–221.

30. Burney, *The Poetry of Our Lord,* p. 91.

31. T. W. Manson, *The Teaching of Jesus,* p. 54.

32. Burney, *The Poetry of Our Lord,* p. 102.

33. *Ibid.,* p. 124.

34. *Ibid.,* p. 148.

35. *Ibid.,* p. 161.

36. T. W. Manson, *The Teaching of Jesus,* p. 56.

37. C. H. Dodd, *Parables of the Kingdom* (Charles Scribner's Sons, 1936), p. 11; Cecil John Cadoux, *The Historic Mission of Jesus,* Lutterworth Library, Vol. 12 (Lutterworth Press, London, 1941), p. 2.

38. Bishop Lowth, *The Sacred Poetry of the Hebrews,* p. 119.

39. C. H. Dodd, *Parables of the Kingdom,* pp. 18, 19.

40. C. H. Dodd rightly emphasizes the historical element in the parables.

41. T. W. Manson, *The Teaching of Jesus,* pp. 69, 70.

42. *Ibid.,* p. 79.

43. Mark 1:22, 27; John Wick Bowman, *The Religion of Maturity* (Abingdon Press, 1948), pp. 275–282.

44. Bowman, *The Intention of Jesus,* p. 99.

45. T. W. Manson, *The Teaching of Jesus,* p. 196; Bowman, *The Intention of Jesus,* pp. 28–40.

46. Sir Edwin C. Hoskyns and F. Noel Davey, *The Fourth Gospel* (Alec R. Allenson, Inc., 1956), Vol. I, pp. 65–70.

47. *Ibid.,* Vol. I, Introduction, p. 4.

48. *Ibid.,* Vol. I, Introduction, p. 90.

49. John Knox, *The Man Christ Jesus* (Harper & Brothers, 1958), pp. 83, 84, 90.

50. Strachan, *The Fourth Gospel,* p. 5.

51. Hoskyns and Davey, *op. cit.,* pp. 512, 513.

52. Strachan, *op. cit.,* pp. 5, 6.

53. Prof. F. C. Grant agrees with Wellhausen and others in attributing the identification between the Suffering Servant and the Son of Man to the primitive Christian community. (*The Earliest Gospel,* p. 74.) Also Wrede, Bultmann, and John Knox.

CHAPTER IV. Jesus Christ

1. Some of the implications of this chapter are brought out in Chapter VII.

CHAPTER V. Contemporary Hindu Thought

1. A. C. Underwood, *Contemporary Thought of India* (Alfred A. Knopf, 1931), p. 196; see also p. 9.

2. Cyril E. M. Joad, *Counter Attack from the East* (W. S. Heinman, 1951), p. 143.

3. Sarvepalli Radhakrishnan, *An Idealist View of Life* (The Macmillan Company, 1932), p. 343.

4. Sarvepalli Radhakrishnan, *The Reign of Religion in Contemporary Philosophy* (Macmillan & Co., Ltd., London, 1920), p. 435.

5. *Ibid.*, p. 443.

6. *Ibid.*, p. 444.

7. Radhakrishnan, *An Idealist View of Life*, p. 344.

8. Radhakrishnan, *The Reign of Religion in Contemporary Philosophy*, p. 444.

9. Radhakrishnan, *An Idealist View of Life*, p. 338.

10. *Ibid.*, p. 332.

11. *Ibid.*

12. *Ibid.*, p. 343.

13. *Ibid.*, p. 340.

14. *Ibid.*, p. 307.

15. Sarvepalli Radhakrishnan, *Eastern Religions and Western Thought* (Oxford University Press, Inc., 1940), p. 44.

16. Radhakrishnan, *An Idealist View of Life*, p. 268.

17. Radhakrishnan, *Eastern Religions and Western Thought*, p. 94.

18. Sarvepalli Radhakrishnan, *The Hindu View of Life* (The Macmillan Company, 1926), p. 75.

19. Radhakrishnan, *An Idealist View of Life*, p. 275.

20. *Ibid.*, p. 276.

21. *Ibid.*, p. 288.

22. Radhakrishnan, *The Hindu View of Life*, pp. 22, 23; Sarvepalli Radhakrishnan, S. Dasgupta, *Philosophical Essays* (University of Calcutta, 1941), p. 385.

23. Radhakrishnan, *Eastern Religions and Western Thought*, p. 49.

24. *Ibid.*, pp. 49, 50.

25. Radhakrishnan, *The Hindu View of Life*, p. 65.

26. Radhakrishnan, *Eastern Religions and Western Thought*, p. 102.

27. Radhakrishnan, *An Idealist View of Life*, p. 339.

28. Sarvepalli Radhakrishnan, *Indian Philosophy* (The Macmillan Company, 1923–1927), Vol. II, pp. 768, 780; *The Hindu View of Life*, p. 130.

29. Sarvepalli Radhakrishnan, *Kalki; or The Future of Civilization* (Hind Kitabs, Ltd., Publishers, Bombay, 1948), pp. 64, 70.

30. S. Dasgupta, *Philosophical Essays*, pp. 225, 226; Radhakrishnan, *Indian Philosophy*, Vol. II, p. 634.

CHAPTER VI. God, the Absolute and the Christ

1. Radhakrishnan, *An Idealist View of Life,* p. 331.
2. *Ibid.,* pp. 333, 109.
3. *Ibid.,* p. 334.
4. *Ibid.,* p. 86.
5. *Ibid.,* p. 338.
6. *Ibid.,* p. 332.
7. *Ibid.,* p. 338.
8. *Ibid.,* pp. 335, 336.
9. *Ibid.,* p. 339.
10. Radhakrishnan, *The Reign of Religion in Contemporary Philosophy,* p. 446.
11. Sarvepalli Radhakrishnan and John Henry Muirhead, eds., *Contemporary Indian Philosophy* (The Macmillan Company, 1952), p. 281.
12. *Ibid.,* p. 280; and Radhakrishnan, *An Idealist View of Life,* p. 342.
13. Radhakrishnan and Muirhead, *Contemporary Indian Philosophy,* p. 285.
14. *Ibid.,* p. 282.
15. *Ibid.,* pp. 281, 282.
16. Radhakrishnan, *An Idealist View of Life,* p. 343.
17. *Ibid.,* p. 344.
18. Radhakrishnan, *Contemporary Indian Philosophy,* p. 286.
19. *Ibid.,* p. 286.
20. Joad, *Counter Attack from the East,* p. 122. Radhakrishnan says "The Divine works and shines through the earthly medium," in Vergilius Ferm, ed., *Religion in Transition* (The Macmillan Company, 1937), p. 40.
21. Radhakrishnan, *An Idealist View of Life,* p. 345.
22. *Ibid.,* p. 86.
23. *Ibid.,* p. 109.
24. *Ibid.,* p. 109.
25. Ferm, *Religion in Transition,* p. 40.
26. *Ibid.,* p. 41.
27. *Ibid.,* p. 4.
28. Radhakrishnan, *Eastern Religions and Western Thought,* p. 22.

29. Radhakrishnan, *An Idealist View of Life,* p. 333.

30. Joad, *Counter Attack from the East,* pp. 117, 118.

31. *Ibid.,* p. 120.

32. Radhakrishnan, *An Idealist View of Life,* p. 109.

33. Radhakrishnan, *The Reign of Religion in Contemporary Philosophy,* p. 443.

34. *Ibid.,* p. vii.

35. Radhakrishnan, *The Hindu View of Life,* p. 66.

36. *Ibid.,* p. 70.

37. Radhakrishnan, *The Reign of Religion in Contemporary Philosophy,* p. 411.

38. *Ibid.,* p. 410.

39. *Ibid.,* p. 443.

40. Robert E. Hume, tr., *The Thirteen Principal Upanishads* (Harper & Brothers, 1954), p. 374.

41. Radhakrishnan, *Eastern Religions and Western Thought,* p. 27.

42. *Ibid.,* p. 44.

43. *Ibid.*

44. *Ibid.,* p. 27.

45. Radhakrishnan, *An Idealist View of Life,* p. 268.

46. *Ibid.,* p. 269.

47. Radhakrishnan, *Indian Philosophy,* Vol. II, p. 604.

48. Radhakrishnan, *Eastern Religions and Western Thought,* p. 26.

49. Radhakrishnan, *An Idealist View of Life,* p. 271.

50. *Ibid.*

51. Radhakrishnan, *Eastern Religions and Western Thought,* p. 31.

52. *Ibid.,* p. 27.

53. E. L. Hinman, *Philosophical Review* (Longmans, Green & Co., Inc., 1921), p. 351.

54. Radhakrishnan, *The Hindu View of Life,* p. 21.

55. Radhakrishnan, *Eastern Religions and Western Thought,* p. 47.

56. Radhakrishnan, *The Reign of Religion in Contemporary Philosophy,* p. ix.

57. Ferm, *Religion in Transition,* p. 35.

58. Radhakrishnan, *The Reign of Religion in Contemporary Philosophy*, pp. 442, 443.

59. *Ibid.*, pp. 448, 449.

60. Radhakrishnan, *An Idealist View of Life*, p. 305.

61. *Ibid.*, p. 306.

62. Joad, *Counter Attack from the East*, p. 211.

63. Radhakrishnan, *Contemporary Indian Philosophy*, p. 285.

64. *Ibid.*, p. 281.

65. Ferm, *Religion in Transition*, p. 41.

66. Radhakrishnan, *The Reign of Religion in Contemporary Philosophy*, p. 445.

67. Hinman, *Philosophical Review*, 1920, p. 584.

68. Radhakrishnan, *Contemporary Indian Philosophy*, p. 282.

69. Radhakrishnan, *The Hindu View of Life*, p. 61.

70. *Ibid.*, p. 76.

71. Ante-Nicene Christian Library, Vol. XII, p. 327.

72. *Ibid.*, Vol. IV, p. 153.

73. Radhakrishnan, *Reign of Religion in Contemporary Philosophy*, p. 444.

74. Where Radhakrishnan held professorship at the time when he published *The Reign of Religion in Contemporary Philosophy*.

75. Hinman, *Philosophical Review*, 1920, p. 586.

76. S. Radhakrishnan, *The Bhagavadgita* (George Allen & Unwin, Ltd., London, 1947).

77. The latest reaffirmation of his credo is found in the volume honoring him in The Library of Living Philosophers, " The Religion of the Spirit and the World's Need: Fragments of a Confession," pp. 5–82 in *The Philosophy of Sarvepalli Radhakrishnan*, edited by Paul Arthur Schilpp (Tudor Publishing Company, 1952).

INDEX

Absolute, the, 129 f., 131, 136, 142, 143 ff.
Adoptionism, 114
Agape, 12–13
Allegro, John, 24
Apollinaris, 112
Aramaic problem, 35
Archegon, 80, 81
Arya Samāj, 168
Athanasius, 11
Authority of Jesus, 89, 90
Avātara, 169, 172

Baillie, D. M., 115–116, 118
Baptism, 54, 90
Barrett, C. K., 58
Barth, Karl, 116–117
Berdyaev, N., 101, 174, 186
Bethune-Baker, J. F., 113
Bhagavadgita, 168
Black, Matthew, 35
Borchert, Otto, 86
Bornkamm, Günther, 33
Bowman, J. W., 86, 89, 90
Brahman-Atman, 132, 151 ff.
Brahmo Samāj, 167–168
Brunner, Emil, 112, 117
Bultmann, R., 32–34, 53, 117
Burney, C. F., 35, 59, 65, 87, 88
Burrows, Millar, 24

Caesarea Philippi, 29, 47
Catechetical schools, 119
Chalcedon, Council of, 37, 104
Charles, R. H., 50
Christ, the, 55
Christianity, 23–25, 27
Christian Science, 18
Clement of Alexandria, 164
Cross, the, 92
Cullmann, O., 23, 25, 26, 52, 67, 118, 119

Dabar, 59
Dalman, G., 35, 48–50, 56
Dead Sea scrolls, 24
Deussen, Paul, 135
Dilthey, W., 33
Divinity of Jesus Christ, 36, 67 ff.
Docetism, 64, 112
Dodd, C. H., 25, 30–32, 35, 38, 59, 64, 67, 88
Dorner, I. A., 120
Dupont-Sommer, André, 24

Elohim, 38
Emerson, Ralph Waldo, 127
Eschatology, 28–31
Essenes, 26
Existentialism, 33, 34